HOW TO MAKE 100

Ribbon Embellishments

Trims, Rosettes, Sculptures, and Baubles for Fashion, Décor, and Crafts

ELAINE SCHMIDT

Creative Publishing
international

Contents

Introduction

Aside from wrapping gifts and tying bows, ribbons can be used for creating trims, braids, rosettes, and other embellishments—from a tailored, pleated medallion that adds a sophisticated decorator touch on a pillow to a fun ribbon sculpture that adds a bit of whimsy on a hair barrette.

Throughout the ages, ribbons have been used as a form of adornment. Even in the Old Testament references are made to "ribbands." During the French Revolution, ribbon cockades were used for designating military personnel. In the 1920s and 1930s, handbooks instructed ladies of the day on how to braid, pleat, fold, gather, smock, and manipulate ribbons into unique accents to make as special gifts or to adorn themselves and their homes. Today there are artists around the world using ribbons in new and exciting ways. In this collection of 100 ribbon embellishment ideas, you'll find projects that use updated, time-honored techniques and contemporary ribbons that are readily available.

You do not need many supplies to make ribbon embellishments; often just ribbon and a bit of thread or glue are all that is required. And the array of ribbons available today is vast, from modern, colorful styles to vintage one-of-a-kind finds. Ribbons in fabric stores, online sewing and quilting websites, and maybe in your own stash of treasures are great sources of inspiration. The techniques needed to make the embellishments are simple, and you are probably already familiar with them if you like to sew and craft.

The ribbon embellishments are divided into four categories: Trims and Braids, Rosettes and Leaves, Ribbon Sculptures, and Beads and Baubles. In the Technical Support chapter (page 138), you will find descriptions of ribbons and the basic materials used to make the embellishments, along with some specialty items that make ribbon work easier and quicker to do than in Victorian times. In this chapter you will also find the basic techniques used for working with ribbons along with a few helpful tips.

This book is designed to be a reference source that you can flip through to find personal favorite embellishment ideas to add to a purchased item or to an original project you are planning to sew or craft. Each embellishment looks very different when made with various sizes, types, and colors of ribbon. Use the instructions I have provided as a starting point and then let your creative juices flow to create your own unique designs. The possibilities are truly endless, so have fun and enjoy creating your own ribbon embellishments.

Trims and Braids

Ribbons can be formed and fashioned in many different ways to create a trim with lots of visual interest. Trims are made by gathering and smocking ribbons or by pleating and folding in simple or intricate patterns to add dimension and texture. Twisted and folded braids, similar to those you may have learned in summer camp, look elegant when made with ribbon. By nature of their construction, some trims are flexible and can be applied around curves. Others are straight and must be positioned flat across a project. Each of the trims included in this section have their own distinctive personality—tailored, frilly, sophisticated, feminine, whimsical, and elegant.

The choice of manufactured trims available to purchase is limited in color and design. By making your own trims from ribbon, you no longer have to settle for what you can find in stores or online. You can choose the perfect ribbon color and trim style to complement any project. Use the instructions and materials suggested as a guide, but consider experimenting with different ribbon types and widths, as well as adding accents such as beads, buttons, lace, or decorative stitching.

GATHERED EDGE TRIM

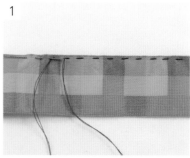

1

2

RIBBONS AND SUPPLIES

soft ribbon that gathers easily, cut to 1½ to 3 times the desired length of the finished trim

thread to match ribbon

needle or sewing machine

Instructions

1. With thread doubled in the needle, hand sew running stitches along one selvage edge of the ribbon. Keep in mind that shorter stitches will make a finer ruffle, while longer stitches will make a fuller ruffle. The stitches can also be sewn by machine.

2. Pull the thread to gather up the ribbon to the desired finished length. Knot thread. Evenly adjust the gathers along the length of the ribbon.

TIPS

• If using a wire-edge ribbon, remove the wire from one side. Carefully pull the wire from the remaining side to gather the ribbon onto the wire. Work slowly from each end and adjust the gathers down toward the center of the ribbon. Secure ends of the ribbon to the wire.
• If you want to make a long length of trim, stop and start the stitching in several places so that the gathering thread does not break when pulled.

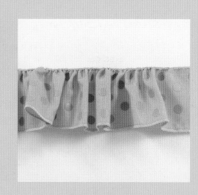

CENTER-GATHERED RUFFLE

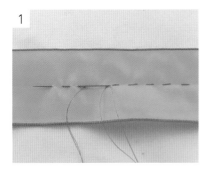

1

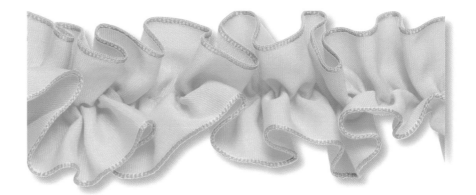

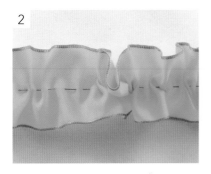

2

Instructions

1. Fold the ribbon in half lengthwise to mark the center. Finger press the fold line as a guide. Hand sew or use a sewing machine to add running stitches down the center of the ribbon.

2. Pull the thread to gather up the ribbon to the desired finished length. Knot thread. Adjust the gathers along the length of the trim, making sure the ribbon does not twist up on itself.

RIBBONS AND SUPPLIES

soft ribbon that gathers easily, cut to 1½ to 4 times the desired length of the finished trim

thread to match ribbon

needle or sewing machine

TIPS

• To make a layered gathered ruffle, center a narrower ribbon on top of a wider one. Pin together and mark center. Then follow steps 1 and 2 above.
• If you want to make a long length of trim, stop and start the stitching in several places so that the gathering thread does not break when pulled.

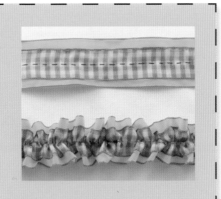

GATHERED CORDING

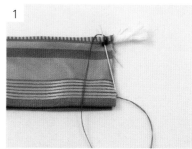

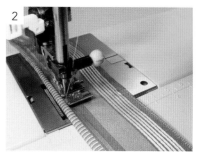

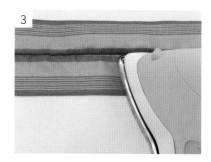

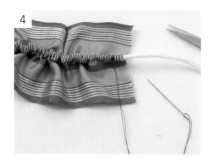

RIBBONS AND SUPPLIES

soft ribbon that gathers easily, 2¼" to 3" (6.5 to 7.5 cm) wide, cut to about two times the desired length of the finished trim

⁵⁄₃₂" (4 mm) cording, cut to match the length of the ribbon plus 3" (7.5 cm)

needle and thread

sewing machine with zipper foot

iron

Instructions

1. Fold the ribbon in half lengthwise, with wrong sides together. Place the cording at the center fold. Secure the end of the cord to the ribbon with a few hand stitches.

2. With the zipper foot attached to the machine, sew a line of straight stitches next to the edge of the cording. Keep the selvage edges of the ribbon even and make sure the cording stays at the center fold. Be careful not to catch the cording in the stitching.

3. Open up the ribbon and gently press the edges flat from the back.

4. Carefully pull the cording to gather the ribbon to the desired length. Distribute gathers evenly down the length of the trim. Secure the end of the cord to the ribbon with a few hand stitches to hold the gathers in place. Trim excess cording.

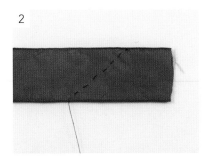

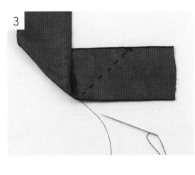

RIBBONS AND SUPPLIES

soft ribbon that gathers easily, any width, cut to 2½ to 4 times the desired length of the finished trim. The exact amount needed will depend upon the thickness of the selected ribbon. The sample shown is made with 1½" (4 cm) taffeta ribbon.

needle and thread

Instructions

1. At one end, fold the ribbon up at a 45-degree angle. Finger press to mark the fold line.

2. Unfold ribbon. From the end of the ribbon, sew running stitches along the fold line.

3. When you reach the opposite edge of the ribbon, fold the ribbon at a 45-degree angle, beginning where the stitches meet the edge. Finger press.

4. Continue sewing along the fold line.

5. Repeat folding and sewing, creating a zigzag line of stitches down the ribbon. Pull up the thread to gather the ribbon. Adjust gathers evenly down the ribbon. Knot the thread at the end to secure.

TIP

The running stitches may also be sewn by machine. Do a small test sample to determine the best stitch length to easily gather the ribbon.

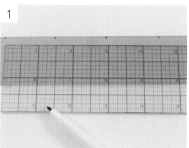

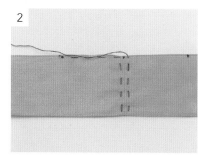

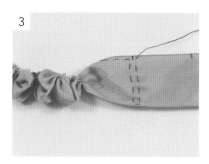

RIBBONS AND SUPPLIES

soft ribbon that gathers easily, ⅞"
(2.2 cm) or wider, cut 2 to 3 times the
desired length of the finished trim.
The exact amount needed depends
upon the thickness of the selected
ribbon. The finished trim will be
about half the width of the ribbon.
The sample shown is made with 1½"
(4 cm) taffeta ribbon.

needle and thread

ruler

fabric marking pen

Instructions

1. Using the marking pen, add small marks along
one selvage side of the ribbon to create the spacing
for the stitching pattern. The marks should be as far
apart as the ribbon is wide. For example, if using a
1½" (4 cm) ribbon, the marks should be 1½" (4 cm)
apart.

2. Starting at the end of the ribbon, sew short running stitches along the edge, stopping just before
the first mark you made with the pen. At this point,
continue the stitches straight across the ribbon to
the other selvage side and then back up a short
distance away.

3. Pull up the thread to gather ribbon and create
the first shell. Continue this stitching pattern down
the length of the ribbon. Pull the thread to form
each shell, making sure that each shell cups in the
same direction.

SCALLOPED-EDGE RUCHING

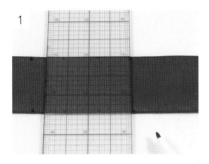

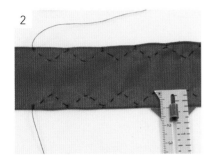

Instructions

1. Using the marking pen, add small marks along both selvage edges to create the spacing for the stitching pattern. Make sure that the marks align and are parallel along both edges. The marks should be as far apart as ½ the width of the ribbon. For example, if using a 1½" (4 cm) ribbon, the marks should be ¾" (2 cm) apart.

2. Sew running stitches along each edge in a zigzag pattern. The stitches should start at the mark on the selvages and angle in between the marks to a halfway point down about ¼ of the width of the ribbon. For a 1½" (4 cm) ribbon, the inside points of the zigzags should be about ⅜" (1 cm) from the edge. It really is not necessary to mark this point, although you can check it with a ruler. Use your eye as a guide as you stitch the zigzag pattern down each edge of the ribbon.

RIBBONS AND SUPPLIES

soft ribbon that gathers easily, ⅞" (2.2 cm) or wider, cut to 3 to 4 times the desired length of the finished trim. The exact amount needed depends on the thickness and softness of the selected ribbon. The sample shown is made with 1½" (4 cm) taffeta ribbon.

needle and thread

ruler

fabric marking pen

3. After several zigzags, pull up both threads simultaneously to gather the ribbon and form the scallops along the edges.

4. Continue to follow the zigzag stitching pattern and gather the ribbon until the trim is the desired length, knotting and adding thread as needed at the selvages. Adjust gathers down the length of the trim.

TIP

If desired, pin the completed trim to your ironing board and apply very light steam to set the gathers and keep the trim flat. Be careful not to flatten the scallops with the iron. Do not set the iron directly on the trim. Hold it above and let the steam penetrate the ribbon. Allow to cool and remove pins.

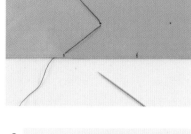

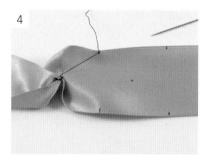

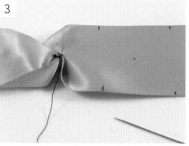

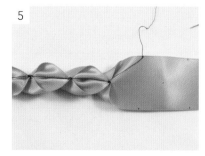

RIBBONS AND SUPPLIES

ribbon, ⅞" (2.2 cm) or 1½" (4 cm) wide, cut to 1½ times the desired length of the finished trim

needle and thread

ruler

fabric marking pen

Instructions

1. On the back side of the ribbon, use the marking pen to add marks along both selvage edges, one ribbon-width apart. The marks will be ⅞" (2.2 cm) apart on ⅞" (2.2 cm) ribbon and 1½" (4 cm) apart on 1½" (4 cm) ribbon. The marks should be parallel. Place marks at the center of the ribbon, halfway between each set of outer marks.

2. Knot thread securely at first outer edge mark. Take a small stitch in the first center mark and another in the opposite outer mark.

3. Pull the three points together and knot securely.

4. Knot thread at the next outer mark, making sure that the thread lies flat between the knots.

5. Repeat steps 2 and 3, working down the ribbon until it is the desired length. This side will be the back side of the trim. Turn the trim over to see the shells and attach the trim to your project.

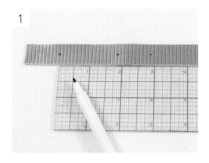

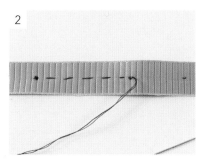

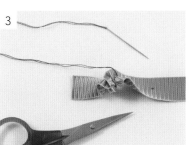

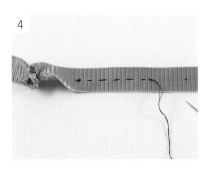

Instructions

1. At the center of the ribbon, use a marking pen to add marks 1⅞" (4.8 cm) apart for the first set of gathers. Place a mark 1" (2.5 cm) away from the last mark for a space. Place marks alternating 1⅞" (4.8 cm) and 1" (2.5 cm) down the length of the ribbon.

2. For the first gathered area, work running stitches along the center of the ribbon between the 1⅞" (4.8 cm) marks.

3. Pull up the thread to gather the ribbon tightly. Securely knot the thread and trim excess.

4. Move along the ribbon 1" (2.5 cm) to the next mark. Repeat steps 2 and 3. Continue this pattern down the length of the ribbon. Twist the gathers neatly into an S shape to form the motifs. The spaces between the gathered motifs should lie flat.

RIBBONS AND SUPPLIES

ribbon, ⅝" (1.5 cm) wide and soft enough to gather easily, cut to 2½ times the desired length of the finished trim

needle and thread

ruler

fabric marking pen

TIP

This trim is made by gathering the ribbon in short areas and then leaving a space between each gathered motif. The sample shown is made with a two-color, double-faced satin ribbon, which provides a pretty effect, as the gathered motifs are a different color than the spaces between them.

RIBBON BEADS TRIM

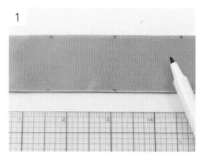

RIBBONS AND SUPPLIES

soft ribbon that gathers easily, ⅞"
(2.2 cm) or 1½" (4 cm) wide, cut to
1¼ times the desired length of the
finished trim

needle and thread

ruler

fabric marking pen

beads or pearls (optional)

Instructions

1. Using a marking pen, add marks along both selvage edges of the ribbon, one ribbon-width apart.
The marks will be ⅞" (2.2 cm) apart on ⅞" (2.2 cm)
ribbon and 1½" (4 cm) apart on 1½" (4 cm) ribbon.
The marks should be parallel.

2. With thread doubled in needle, insert needle into
the ribbon at the first mark. Sew running stitches
across the width of the ribbon, stopping at the
opposite mark.

3. Pull up the thread to gather the ribbon. Bring the
needle around the back of the ribbon to the first
mark and pull stitches tight. Wrap thread around
the gathered area a few times and secure thread.

4. If desired, sew a bead or pearl over the gathers.

5. Continue sewing running stitches across the
ribbon, matching opposite marks, to create a line
of ribbon "beads" down the length of the ribbon. If
desired, the gathered beads can be lightly stuffed
with batting or cotton balls as the trim is stitched to
your finished project.

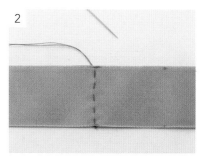

SEMICIRCLES

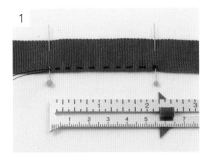

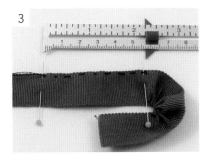

RIBBONS AND SUPPLIES

soft ribbon that gathers easily, ⅝"
to 1½" (1.5 cm to 4 cm) wide, cut
to 3 times the desired length of the
finished trim

needle and thread

ruler

pins

Instructions

1. Starting an inch or so from the cut end of the
ribbon, with thread doubled in needle, sew a line
of running stitches along one selvage edge of the
ribbon. Make the length of the stitching 3 times the
width of the ribbon. For example, on a ¾" (2 cm)
ribbon, the line of stitching should be 2¼" (6 cm)
long. Use a ruler and pin to mark the desired length
of the stitching.

2. Pull thread tightly to gather the ribbon. Knot end
securely and trim excess thread.

3. On the opposite edge of the ribbon, insert a pin
at the same point of the last stitch on the beginning
side. Sew a line of running stitches along the selvage edge. Make the length of the stitching 3 times
the width of the ribbon. Use a ruler and pin to mark
the desired length of the stitching.

4. Pull thread tightly to gather the ribbon. Knot
end securely and trim excess. Repeat the pattern,
alternating stitching along the selvages from side
to side. The ribbon will curve into an S shape.

5. To create a ruffled edge trim, fold every other
semi-circle up so all the curves are on one side of
the trim.

WRAPPED CANDY RIBBON TRIM

RIBBONS AND SUPPLIES

soft ribbon that gathers easily, 2¼" to 3" (5.5 cm to 7.5 cm) wide, cut to about two times the desired length of the finished trim

needle and thread

ruler

pins

Pleats, gathered at both ends, form rows of "wrapped candy" down the length of a wide ribbon.

Instructions

1. Fold the beginning end of the ribbon, wrong sides together, about 2" (5 cm) from the end. Place a pin ¾" (2 cm) parallel from the fold line. Sew a line of small running stitches along the pin, starting and stopping the stitching ½" (1.3 cm) from each edge of the ribbon. Secure thread at the end and trim excess.

2. Finger-press the pleat into a cylinder. Sew running stitches across one end of the cylinder. Be careful to only catch one layer of ribbon as you sew.

3. Pull up stitches to tightly gather the end of the cylinder. Secure thread and trim excess.

4. Sew running stitches across the other end of the cylinder and pull to gather. Secure thread and trim excess.

5. Continue to create pleats, forming them into gathered cylinders, down the length of the ribbon. Evenly space the pleats about 2" (5 cm) apart.

1

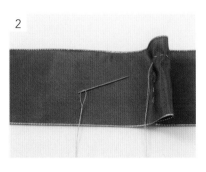

2

3

4

5

TIP

Make the cylinders wider by increasing the distance between the stitching line and the fold. Feel free to place the cylinders closer together or wider apart. If you are using a striped or plaid ribbon, you can follow the pattern lines for placement of the pleats.

KNIFE-PLEAT TRIM

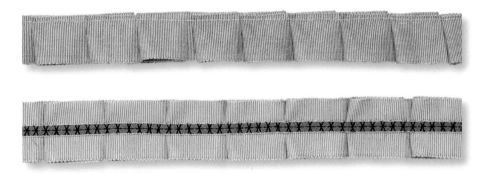

RIBBONS AND SUPPLIES

ribbon of any width, cut to about
3 times the desired length of the
finished trim

ruler

pins

fabric marking pen (optional)

needle and thread or sewing machine

iron (optional)

Instructions

1. A knife-pleat trim is made with all the pleats folded in the same direction. Use pins or a fabric marking pen to mark the pleat placement lines along one edge of the ribbon. Place the marks one ribbon-width apart. For example, if you have selected a 1" (2.5 cm) ribbon, mark the ribbon every 1" (2.5 cm).

2. Fold the ribbon, wrong sides together, at the third mark from the end. Bring the fold line up to meet the first mark. Align ribbon edges and pin the newly formed pleat.

3. To make the next pleat, fold the ribbon, wrong sides together, at the third mark after the first fold. Bring the fold line up to meet the first mark after the first pleat. Align edges and pin second pleat.

4. By hand or with a machine, stitch along the edge of the ribbon to hold the pleats in place. Continue to fold and pin and stitch the pleats down the length of the ribbon. If you are using pins instead of a fabric marking pen, measure and add more pins as you pleat the ribbon.

5. Press the pleats flat or leave them unpressed for a softer look.

1

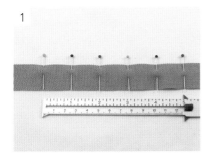

2

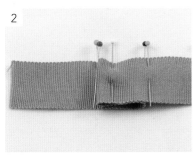

3

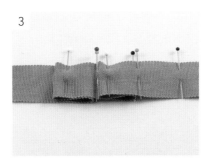

4

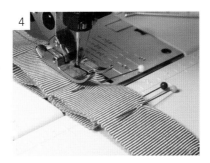

5

TIP

The ribbon can be sewn down the center. If desired, the stitching can be covered with a narrow ribbon or trim and/or decorative stitches.

• Vary the width and spacing of the pleats. The pleats can be narrower or deeper and can be closer together or farther apart. Make a test sample to calculate the necessary ribbon yardage required for the pleat pattern you desire.

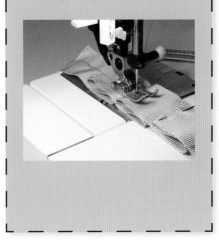

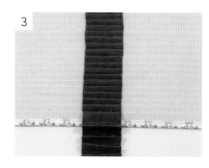

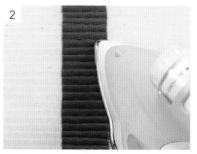

RIBBONS AND SUPPLIES

ribbon ⅝" (1.5 cm) or wider, such as petersham, that will hold pleats well when pressed, cut to 3½ times the desired length of the finished trim.

pleater board

thin ruler or credit card

iron

pressing cloth

white vinegar

water-soluble tape (optional)

TIP

Different size pleats can be made by tucking the ribbon into every other or every third louver of the pleater.

Accordion pleats are very narrow knife pleats, and they are difficult to form as instructed for basic Knife Pleat Trim on page 22. A pleater board makes it easy to fold the ribbon and set the pleats.

Instructions

1. Following the manufacturer's instructions, tuck the ribbon into each louver of the pleater. Use a ruler or credit card to push the ribbon all the way down into each louver.

2. Use a damp pressing cloth to help set the pleats. Mix a solution of 1 part white vinegar to 9 parts water and dip the pressing cloth into the solution. Wring out the cloth and place it over the tucked ribbon and press with an iron set to high heat. Remove cloth and press again.

3. Once the ribbon has cooled completely, remove it from the pleater. Tuck the last pleat made into the first louver and continue to pleat the ribbon across the pleater. Tuck and press pleats down the ribbon until the pleated trim is the desired length.

4. The pleated ribbon can be sewn along one edge or down the middle of the trim. Before removing the pleated ribbon from the pleater, apply water-soluble tape to temporarily hold the pleats before stitching.

SCALLOPED ACCORDION PLEATS

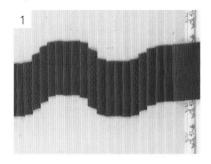

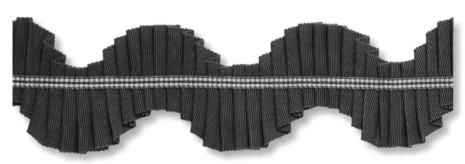

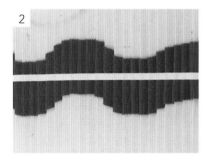

Instructions

1. Follow the instructions on opposite page for making Accordion Pleats. Tuck the ribbon into the first three louvers of the pleater. Holding these pleats in place, tuck the next three pleats "up the hill" at a 45-degree angle. Straighten the ribbon and tuck the next three pleats straight. Tuck the next three pleats "down the hill" at a 45-degree angle. Continue this pattern across the pleater. Press and cool.

2. Following the manufacturer's instructions, apply a strip of fusible web tape down the center of the ribbon to hold the pleats in place.

3. When cool, remove the ribbon from the pleater. Tuck the last pleat made into the first louver and continue to follow the pattern to scallop pleat the ribbon across the pleater. Apply fusible web tape before removing the ribbon from the pleater. Continue to make pleats and apply fusible web tape down the ribbon until it is the desired length.

4. Remove paper backing from tape. Fuse narrow ribbon to pleated ribbon. Sew narrow ribbon to pleated ribbon.

RIBBONS AND SUPPLIES

ribbon ⅝" (1.5 cm) or wider, such as petersham, that will hold pleats well when pressed, cut to 3½ times the desired length of the finished trim

⅛" (3 mm) ribbon cut the desired length of the finished trim

pleater board

thin ruler or credit card

iron

pressing cloth

white vinegar

⅛" (3 mm) fusible web tape

sewing machine and thread

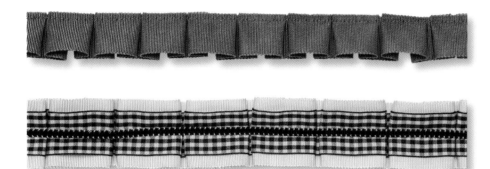

RIBBONS AND SUPPLIES

ribbon, any width, cut to about
3 times the desired length of the
finished trim

ruler

pins

fabric marking pen (optional)

needle and thread or sewing machine

iron (optional)

Instructions

1. Box pleats are made with the under edges folded toward the center of each pleat, creating a box shape on the front. Use pins or a fabric marking pen to mark the pleat placement lines along one edge of the ribbon. Place the marks one ribbon-width apart. For example, if you have selected a 1" (2.5 cm) ribbon, mark the ribbon every 1" (2.5 cm).

2. To make the first half of the box pleat, bring the second mark from the end of the ribbon up to meet the first mark. Fold, align ribbon edges, and pin.

3. To make the second half of the box pleat, match up the next two marks with right sides together. Fold up the pleat formed at the back of the ribbon. The fold lines of the two halves will meet at the center back of the "box." Align ribbon edges and pin to complete one box pleat.

4. Continue to follow this pattern to fold pleats in the ribbon. Pin or baste to hold. By hand or machine, stitch along the edge of the ribbon.

5. Press the pleats flat or leave them unpressed for a softer look.

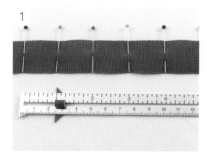

1

4

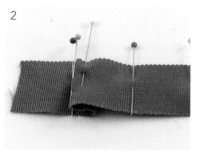

2

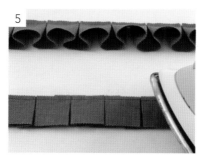

5

3

TIPS

• The ribbon can be sewn down the center. Cover the stitching with a narrow ribbon, trim, or decorative stitches. The double layer sample shown is made with a narrower ribbon sewn on top of a wider ribbon before the pleats were folded.

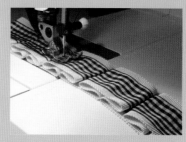

• Vary the width and spacing of the pleats. The pleats can be narrower or deeper and can be closer together or farther apart. Make a test sample to calculate the necessary ribbon yardage required for the pleat pattern you desire.

DOUBLE BOX PLEATS

RIBBONS AND SUPPLIES

ribbon, ⅞" (2.2 cm) or wider, cut to
about 5 times the desired length of
the finished trim

ruler

pins

fabric marking pen

needle and thread

sewing machine (optional)

Instructions

1. Double box pleats are made with two folded
pleats on each side of the center box shape. Review
the instructions for making Box Pleat Trim on page
26. Place marks for fold lines one ribbon-width
apart. When working with an evenly woven check
ribbon such as the sample shown, count the squares
of the check instead of marking the ribbon to position the fold lines.

2. To make the left half of the double box pleat,
bring the second mark from the end of the ribbon
up to meet the first mark. Fold, align ribbon edges,
and pin. Bring the next mark up to meet the fold
line of the first half of the left pleat. Reposition pin
to hold.

3. To make the right half of the double box pleat,
match up the next two marks, right sides together.
Fold up the pleat formed at the back of the ribbon.
The fold lines of the two halves will meet at the
center back of the "box." Align ribbon edges and
pin. Bring the next mark up to meet the fold line of
the first half of the right side of the double pleat.
Reposition pin to hold. One complete double box
pleat has been formed.

4. Continue to fold double box pleats down the
length of the ribbon. Machine stitch close to one
edge of the ribbon to hold the pleats.

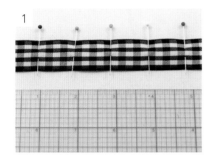

1

2

3

4

TIPS

• Double box pleats can also be sewn down the center of the ribbon with straight or decorative stitches.

• Triple box pleats can be formed by making three folds on each side of the center of the pleat. You would need to cut the ribbon 7 times the desired length of the finished trim.

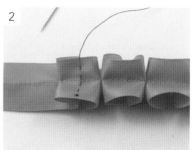

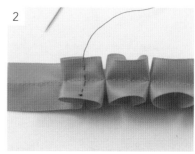

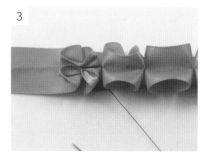

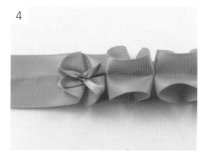

RIBBONS AND SUPPLIES

soft ribbon that gathers easily, ⅞"
to 1½" (2.2 cm to 4 cm) wide, cut to
about 3 times the desired length of
the finished trim

ruler

pins

fabric marking pen

sewing machine

needle and thread

small beads

Instructions

1. Follow instructions for the Box Pleat Trim on
page 26. Pin box pleats down the length of the ribbon. Machine stitch down the center of the ribbon
to hold the pleats.

2. Insert threaded needle into one side of the center box of the first pleat. Sew running stitches across
the center of the pleat, ending at the opposite
edge of the pleat. Take care that the thread only
goes through the top ribbon of the pleat.

3. Pull up stitches to tightly gather the top of the
pleat. Bring edges of pleat together and secure
with a stitch to the center of the pleat.

4. Sew a bead to the center of the gathered rose-
bud. Bring needle to the back of the ribbon, secure
thread and trim.

5. Continue to gather and add a bead to each pleat
of the trim.

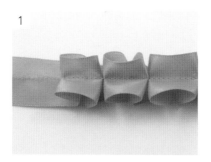

PULLED BOX PLEATS

1

2

3

Instructions

1. Follow the instructions on page 28 for making Double Box Pleats. Mark the pleat fold lines one ribbon-width apart. If the ribbon is an evenly woven check, as the sample shown, count the squares of the check instead of marking the ribbon to position the fold lines.

2. On the back side of the ribbon, sew the pleat fold lines to the center of the box pleat with a few stitches to hold. Knot thread and trim.

3. Fold and stitch double box pleats down the length of the ribbon.

4. At the center of each pleat, pull the edges of the top ribbon layer together and sew with a few small stitches. Knot thread and trim.

RIBBONS AND SUPPLIES

ribbon, ⅞" (2.2 cm) or wider, cut to about 5 times the length of the desired finished trim

ruler

pins

fabric marking pen

needle and thread

4

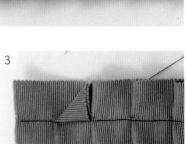

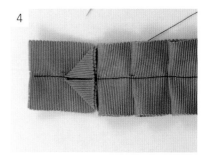

RIBBONS AND SUPPLIES

ribbon, ⅞" (2.2 cm) or wider, cut to 3 times the desired length of the finished trim

ruler

fabric marking pen

pins

needle and thread

sewing machine (optional)

Instructions

1. Follow instructions for Knife Pleat Trim on page 22. Mark placement lines at the center of the ribbon for making knife pleats half the width of the selected ribbon. The sample shown is made with 1½" (4 cm) ribbon, and the marks are placed ¾" (2 cm) apart.

2. Fold pleats and pin. Machine stitch down the center of the ribbon. If you prefer, hand-tack each pleat at the center to hold.

3. Beginning at the first pleat, fold one outer edge of the pleat foldline down to the center of the ribbon. Secure with a stitch. Do not cut thread.

4. Fold other edge of pleat foldline down to the center of the pleat, forming a triangle. Stitch to hold center points together. Secure thread at the back.

5. Repeat steps 2 and 3 with all the knife pleats down the length of the ribbon. You do not need to cut the thread between each triangle. Secure the thread with a stitch so that it remains flat against the back of the ribbon and is not pulled too tightly. The points of each triangle should touch the base of the adjacent triangle.

DIAMONDS AND SQUARES

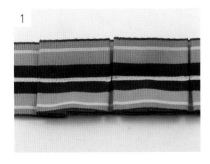

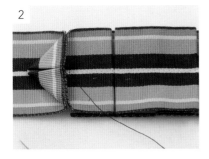

This technique produces different effects depending on the ribbon selected. A solid ribbon will show off the folded diamond motifs. A striped ribbon, as used in the sample shown, will form an interesting geometric pattern with squares formed by the stripes between the folded diamonds.

Instructions

1. Follow the instructions for the Box Pleat Trim on page 26. Mark the ribbon down the center. The marks should be as far apart as the width of the ribbon. Pin box pleats down the length of the ribbon. Machine stitch down the center of the ribbon to hold the pleats. Press box pleats flat.

2. Starting at the first pleat, fold the two outer corners of the left side of the pleat to the center. Secure with a few stitches. Do not cut thread.

3. Fold the two outer corners of the right side of the pleat to the center. Secure with a few stitches. One diamond motif has been formed. Bring thread to the back, knot, and trim excess.

4. Continue to fold the corners of all pleats to form a row of diamond motifs down the length of the ribbon.

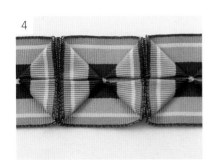

RIBBONS AND SUPPLIES

ribbon, 1½" (4 cm) or wider, cut to about 3 times the desired length of the finished trim

ruler

pins

fabric marking pen

sewing machine

iron

needle and thread

TIP

Space the pleats farther apart to create a Diamonds and Rectangles pattern.

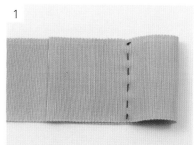

1

RIBBONS AND SUPPLIES

ribbon, 1½" (4 cm) or wider, cut to 3 times the desired length of the finished trim

needle and thread

ruler

pins

Instructions

1. Starting a few inches from one end of the ribbon, fold the ribbon in half, wrong sides together. Stitch across the width of the ribbon ⅔ of the ribbon width away from the fold. (For example, on a 1½" [4 cm] ribbon, stitch 1" [2.5 cm] from the fold.)

2. Open the pleat formed on the right side of the ribbon. Pinching it at the fold line, fold the pleat into three equally sized pleats. Sew the pleats together at the center of the ribbon.

3. To form the bows, spread the pleats open and sew the corners of the outer edges of the outside pleats to the base ribbon. The corners will curve inward and should be stitched slightly away from the selvage edges.

4. Evenly fold and sew pleats down the ribbon, forming each into a bow.

2

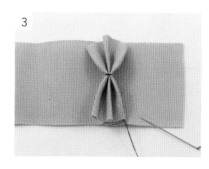

3

4

BOW TIES

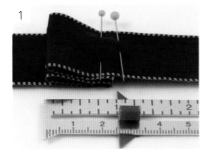

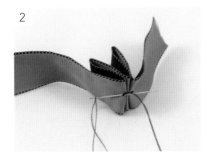

A two-color double-sided ribbon is especially attractive for this technique as both sides will show on the finished trim.

Instructions

1. Starting a few inches from one end of the ribbon, make a stack of two pleats. The pleats should be as deep as the width of the ribbon. For example, make the pleats 1" (2.5 cm) wide on a 1" (2.5 cm) ribbon. Use a ruler and pins to measure each pleat.

2. To hold the pleats on the wrong side of the ribbon, sew the folds together at the center. There will be three folds on the wrong side.

3. On the right side, place one pleat to the left and one to the right.

4. Overlap the selvage edges at the center of the pleat and secure with a stitch.

RIBBONS AND SUPPLIES

ribbon, ⅞" (2.2 cm) or wider, cut to 3½ times the desired length of the finished trim

needle and thread

ruler

pins

small buttons, beads, ribbon roses, or other small embellishment

5. Sew a button or other small embellishment to the center of the pleat.

6. Move along the ribbon one ribbon width from the edge of the completed bow tie to begin another set of pleats.

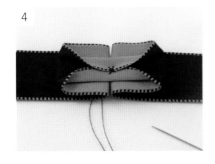

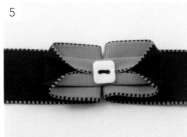

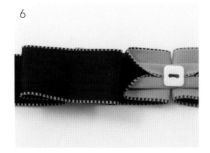

PADDLEWHEEL TRIM

RIBBONS AND SUPPLIES

ribbon that makes crisp pleats,
such as grosgrain or petersham;
⅞" (2.2cm) or wider, cut 5
to 6 times the desired length of
the finished trim

needle and thread

ruler

pins

binder clip or clothes pin

Instructions

1. A few inches from one end of the ribbon, fold six pleats, making them all the same size. The pleats should be half the width of the ribbon. The ribbon shown is 1½" (4 cm) and the pleats are ¾" (2 cm) deep. Hold them together with a binder clip or clothes pin.

2. Turn the ribbon over. There will be seven pleats on the wrong side of the trim. Insert the double threaded needle just into each fold at the center and sew the pleats together. Pull pleats close and knot thread. In the same way, sew the pleats together at both selvage edges.

3. Turn the trim to the right side. Remove clip or pin. Flatten ribbon and fan out pleats.

4. Tuck both edges of each pleat into the center of the pleat. A small pair of sharp scissors is helpful for turning in the ribbon edges.

5. Stitch through all the folds near both selvages of the ribbon.

6. One paddle wheel has been completed. Move along the ribbon one-and-one-half times the width of the ribbon to begin the next paddlewheel. Evenly space the paddlewheels down the ribbon or vary the spacing as desired.

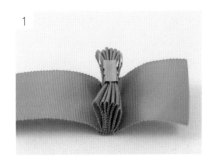

1

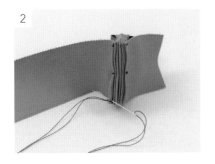

2

3

4

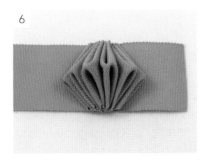

5

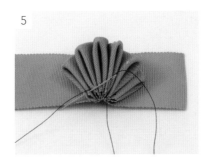

6

RIBBONS AND SUPPLIES

ribbon, ⅞" (2.2 cm) wide, cut to
2½ times the desired length of the
finished trim

ruler

iron

needle and thread

*Select striped grosgrain ribbon for making this trim,
as the woven stripes show off the pattern of the folds.*

Instructions

1. At one end of the ribbon, fold the long working
end of the ribbon up at a 45-degree angle. Press.
This will be the back side of the trim.

2. Continuing to work with the long end, fold the
ribbon down and around to the front of the trim to
create a triangle. Press.

3. Fold the working end straight up and across the
back side of the trim. Press.

4. Fold the working end down at a 45-degree angle,
placing it inside the fold created in step 3. Press.
The diagonal lines created in steps 1 and 3 will align
on the back side of the trim.

5. Slipstitch the diagonal lines together to secure
the folds.

6. Moving over ⅞" (2.2 cm), fold the working end
of the ribbon up at a 45-degree angle and follow
the steps above to create the next block. Fold and
stitch blocks down the length of the ribbon.

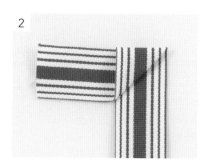

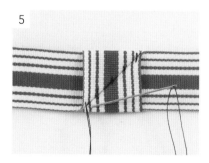

1

2

3

4

5

Consider using a striped ribbon for this trim, as it will create an interesting pattern when folded.

RIBBONS AND SUPPLIES

ribbon that makes crisp pleats, such as grosgrain or petersham, 1½" (4 cm) wide, cut to 2½ times the desired length of the finished trim

needle and thread

ruler

pins

iron

Instructions

1. Fold back the ribbon a few inches from one end with wrong sides together and pin. Sew a line of stitches, selvage to selvage, ¾" (2 cm) from the fold, to create a pleat.

2. Press the pleat open, creating a box pleat.

3. Fold the selvage edge from the top layer of the bottom side of the pleat up to the center. Sew the point to the center of the pleat with a small stitch.

4. Fold the other selvage edge of the pleat down to the center and secure with a stitch. The two folds should meet at the center, creating a hexagon.

5. Continue to make pleats, forming hexagons down the ribbon. Fold each pleat 2¼" (5.5 cm) from the fold line of the previous pleat.

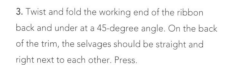

RIBBONS AND SUPPLIES

ribbon, ⅞" (2.2 cm) or wider, cut 2 to 2½ times the desired length of the finished trim

iron

needle and thread

Instructions

1. With the wrong side of the ribbon facing up, fold up the end of the ribbon at a 45-degree angle and press.

2. Fold up the longer end of the ribbon at a 45-degree angle, creating a point facing downward. The selvages should be straight and right next to each other at the center of the point. Press.

3. Twist and fold the working end of the ribbon back and under at a 45-degree angle. On the back of the trim, the selvages should be straight and right next to each other. Press.

4. Fold down the working end of the ribbon at a 45-degree angle, creating a point facing upward. The selvages should be straight and right next to each other at the center of the point. Press.

5. Twist and fold the working end of the ribbon back and under at a 45-degree angle and press.

6. Repeat steps 2–5 to fold down the length of the ribbon. To hold the twists in place, sew each fold at the center of the trim with a few small stitches. Use either side of the trim as the "right" side.

PRAIRIE POINTS

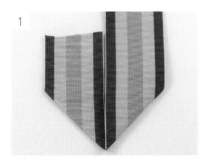

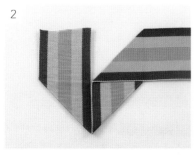

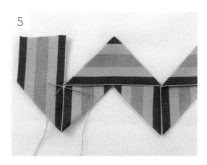

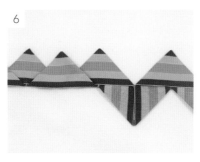

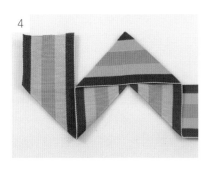

RIBBONS AND SUPPLIES

ribbon, ⅞" (2.2 cm) or wider, cut to 2 to 2½ times the desired length of the finished trim

iron

needle and thread

3. Twist and fold the working end of the ribbon to the back at a 45-degree angle, creating a point that faces up. On the back of the trim, the selvages should be straight and right next to each other at the center of the point. Press.

4. Twist and fold the working end of the ribbon back and under at a 45-degree angle.

5. Follow steps 2–4 to fold alternating points down the length of the ribbon. The down points will have the selvages showing at the center. The up points will have the selvages at the back. To hold the twists in place, sew each fold at the center of the trim with a few small stitches.

6. Fold the alternating down points up along the center line of the trim so that all the triangles point in the same direction. If desired, secure the folds with a few stitches to hold the trim flat.

Instructions

1. Follow steps 1 and 2 opposite for making Zigzag Trim. The first point folded will point down.

2. Fold the working end of the ribbon down and to the front at a 45-degree angle. Press.

RIBBONS AND SUPPLIES

ribbon, ⅝" to 1" (1.5 cm to 2.5 cm) wide, cut to 3½ times the desired length of the finished trim

pins

iron

needle and thread

To show off the changing directions of the folds in this trim, choose a two-color double-sided ribbon.

Instructions

1. Starting at one end, fold ribbon down at a 45-degree angle. Pin and press.

2. Fold ribbon to the back and straight up to form the first triangle fold. Pin and press.

3. Fold ribbon to the left at a 45-degree angle. Pin and press. The selvage edge of the working end of the ribbon will be parallel to the selvage edge of the beginning end.

4. Fold ribbon to the back and to the right to form the second triangle fold. Pin and press. With a few small stitches, secure folds at the tip of the triangle.

5. Repeat step 1, folding ribbon down at a 45-degree angle. The selvage edge of the working end of the ribbon should be parallel to the selvage edge of the first folded square.

6. Repeat steps 2 to 4. Continue to follow steps 1 to 4, folding triangles down the length of the ribbon and stitching each fold with a few small stitches to hold the ribbon in place.

1

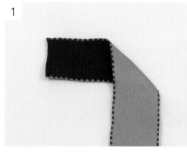

2

3

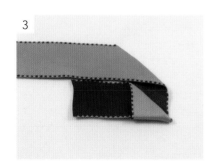

4

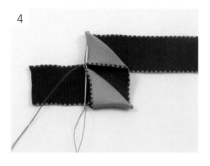

5

TIPS

• Pin the ribbon to an ironing board as the ribbon is twisted and folded. Press each fold as you form and stitch it.

• The trim can be made from a solid color ribbon, or two different ribbons can be fused or held together as one.

WOVEN RIBBON BAND

RIBBONS AND SUPPLIES

ribbon, ⅝" (1.5 cm) wide, for the lengthwise rows. Cut three lengths the desired length of the finished trim, plus 1" (2.5 cm).

ribbon, ⅝" (1.5 cm) wide, for the crosswise rows, cut to 5½ times the desired length of the finished trim

fusible interfacing, cut 1⅞" (4.7 cm) wide to the desired length of the finished trim

pins

pinable surface such as an ironing board or piece of foam core

iron

sewing machine

thread to match ribbon

For this embellishment, select a ribbon that is the same on both sides, as both sides will show when woven.

Instructions

1. Place fusible interfacing strip, adhesive side up, on pinable surface. Pin three lengthwise ribbons to the end of the interfacing, keeping the ribbons parallel and the edges next to each other.

2. For first row, weave crosswise ribbon, working over outer ribbons and under middle ribbon. Pin.

3. Fold ribbon into a point and pin. For second row, weave ribbon under outer ribbons and over middle ribbon. Pin.

4. Continue to weave these two alternating rows down the length of the fusible interfacing, folding and pinning the ribbon at each turning point and keeping the rows parallel.

5. Following the manufacturer's instructions, iron interfacing to woven ribbons, removing pins as it is fused. Sew a line of stitching down each edge of the woven band to secure all ribbon rows.

1

2

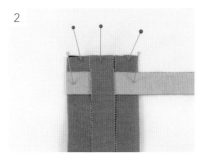

3

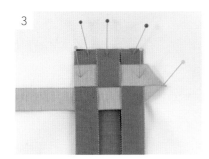

4

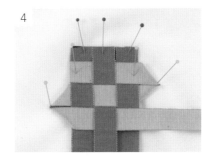

5

TIP

The band can be woven with different widths of ribbon. The number of lengthwise rows can be increased. Cut the interfacing strip the total width of the lengthwise ribbon rows. Make a sample to test the yardage needed to weave the desired length of the band.

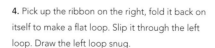

RIBBONS AND SUPPLIES

ribbon, ⅛" to ⅜" (3 mm to 1 cm) wide. Depending upon the width of the ribbon, you will need up to 10 times the desired length of the finished trim.

needle and thread or fabric glue

When selecting ribbon for the looped braid trim, keep in mind that both sides of the ribbon will show when the trim is braided.

Instructions

1. Hold the ribbon at the center and form a loop by crossing the right ribbon over the left.

2. With the ribbon coming from the top of the cross, make a flat loop by folding the ribbon back on itself, wrong sides together. Slip loop into the first loop.

3. Draw the loops together snugly, down to the ribbon width.

4. Pick up the ribbon on the right, fold it back on itself to make a flat loop. Slip it through the left loop. Draw the left loop snug.

5. Continue in this pattern, creating a loop with the left ribbon and then one with the right, until the braid is the desired length.

6. To finish the braid, pull the end of one ribbon through the last loop. Trim ends. Stitch or glue ribbons to secure.

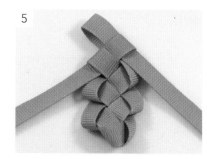

TWO-COLOR LOOPED BRAID

Instructions: Variation 1

1. With double-sided ribbon, follow instructions opposite for making a Looped Braid. One color of ribbon will be on the sides of the braid and the other color will be in the center.

2. If using two different colors of ribbons, hold them together back to back as one ribbon, with right sides out. Follow instructions for making a Looped Braid.

Instructions: Variation 2

1. Use a needle and thread to hand-tack a loop at the end of each ribbon, creating an opening equal to the ribbon width. Hold one ribbon in each hand and slip the right loop through the left loop.

2. Braid the ribbons, following the instructions for making a Looped Braid. One color of ribbon will be on the left edge and the other color will be on the right edge.

RIBBONS AND SUPPLIES

Variation 1: double-sided satin ribbon, ⅛" to ⅜" (3 mm to 1 cm) wide, with different colors on each side, or two ribbons of the same width in different colors. Depending upon the width of the selected ribbons, you will need to cut each ribbon up to 10 times the desired length of the finished trim.

Variation 2: ribbon in two colors, ⅛" to ⅜" (3 mm to 1 cm) wide. Depending upon the width of the selected ribbon, you will need to cut each ribbon up to 5 times the desired length of the desired finished trim.

needle and thread or fabric glue

RIBBONS AND SUPPLIES

ribbon, ⅜" (1 cm) wide, cut to 8 times the desired length of the finished length of the trim

needle and thread

Instructions

1. Form a ⅜" (1 cm) loop at one end of the ribbon. Secure the loop with a few stitches. Knot and trim excess thread.

2. Hold the long end of the ribbon to the back and form a new loop by folding the ribbon in half.

3. Place the new loop through the previous loop. Adjust the size of the new loop to ⅜" (1 cm).

4. Holding the long end of the ribbon to the back, form another loop by folding the ribbon in half.

5. Place this loop through the previous loop. Adjust the size to ⅜" (1 cm).

6. Continue in this pattern, working from side to side, bringing the ribbon to the back, folding a loop and pushing it through the previous loop. Each time, make sure to adjust the size of the loop to ⅜" (1 cm). When the rick rack is the desired length, slip the end of the ribbon through the final loop. The side of the rick rack facing you will be the front of the rick rack, as it is slightly neater than the back.

1

2

3

4

5

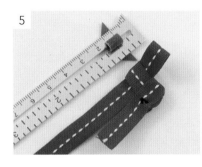

6

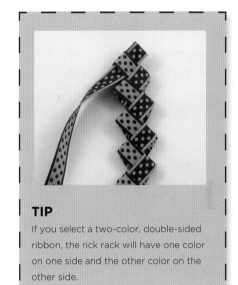

TIP

If you select a two-color, double-sided ribbon, the rick rack will have one color on one side and the other color on the other side.

TWISTED RIBBON CORD

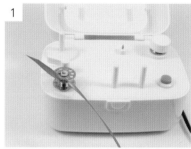

RIBBONS AND SUPPLIES

ribbon, ⅛" to ¼" (3 mm to 6 mm) wide, cut to 2½ times the desired length of the finished cord

sewing machine or stand-alone bobbin winder

sewing machine bobbin

Instructions

1. Cut the end of the ribbon into a long point. Thread it through one hole in the bobbin and secure with an overhand knot. Place the bobbin into the sewing machine bobbin winder or the stand-alone winder, with the tied ribbon end facing out.

2. Hold the free ribbon end taut in one hand, keeping it away from the bobbin. Start the winder and the ribbon will twist tightly up the length. Make sure to hold the ribbon away from the bobbin and do not let the ribbon wind onto the bobbin.

3. Stop the winder. Keeping the tension on the end of the ribbon with one hand, grasp the twisted ribbon at the half-way point with the other hand. Bring the end to the bobbin so the ribbon is folded in half. Release the half-way point, and the ribbon will twist upon itself to form a cord. Tie the ends together in an overhand knot to keep the twists in place.

4. Cut the cord from the bobbin winder.

TIP
Before twisting the cord, consider combining crochet and embroidery threads, as well as strands of small beads with the ribbons.

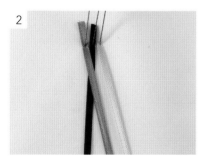

RIBBONS AND SUPPLIES

ribbon, ⅛" (3 mm) wide in one or three colors, each cut to a length 1¼ times the desired length of the finished trim

pins

pinable surface such as an ironing board or piece of foam core

needle and thread

This trim is braided with three lengths of ribbon. Each can be a different color for a tri-color trim or all three lengths can be the same color for a one-color trim.

Instructions

1. Pin the ends of the ribbon lengths side-by-side to the board.

2. Pass the left ribbon over the middle ribbon.

3. Pass the right ribbon over the middle ribbon.

4. Continue in this pattern, pinning the ribbons to keep them right-side up and relatively flat.

5. Stitch the ribbon lengths at each end to secure. Carefully iron braid flat. To make a length of braid longer than the board, braid to the end of the board. Secure beginning ends. Unpin and move the completed trim up the board. Repin at the top and continue braiding.

RIBBONS AND SUPPLIES

ribbon, ¼" to ⅜" (6 mm to 1 cm) wide, in one or three colors, each cut to a length 1¼ times the desired length of the finished trim.

pins

pinable surface such as an ironing board or piece of foam core

needle and thread

This trim is braided with three lengths of ribbon. Each can be a different color for a tri-color trim or all three lengths can be the same color. Both sides of the ribbon will show when the trim is braided.

Instructions

1. Pin the ends of the ribbon lengths side-by-side to the board. Pass the left ribbon over the middle ribbon. Pass the right ribbon over the middle ribbon.

2. Continue this pattern, folding each outside ribbon over and toward the middle ribbon. Pin the ribbons to the board as you braid.

3. Keep an even tension on all three ribbons. The outer edges should form straight lines to create an even width trim.

4. Stitch the ribbon lengths at each end to secure. Carefully iron braid flat. To make a length of braid longer than the board, braid to the end of the board. Secure beginning ends. Unpin and move the completed trim up the board. Repin at the top and continue braiding.

1

2

3

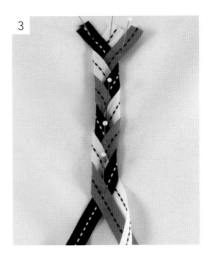

TIPS

• If you select ribbons that are different colors on the front and the back, an interesting variegated pattern will emerge as you braid.

• Wider ribbons, if they are soft enough, can be braided. Gather the lengths in your hands as you pass the ribbons over each other. Tighten the ribbons so the braid lies flat and even in width.

FOLDED FOUR-PLY BRAID

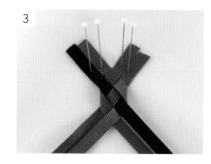

RIBBONS AND SUPPLIES

ribbon, ¼" to ⅜" (6 mm to 1 cm) wide in one, two, or four colors, each cut to a length 1½ times the desired length of the finished trim

pins

pinable surface such as an ironing board or piece of foam core

needle and thread

This braid can be made from one, two, or four colors of ribbon. Both sides of the ribbon will show when the trim is braided.

Instructions

1. Pin the ends of the ribbon lengths in sets of two at right angles to each other. Weave the center right ribbon over the center left ribbon and under the outer left ribbon. Weave the outer right ribbon under the center left ribbon and over the outer left ribbon.

2. Fold the outer left ribbon over to the right, at right angles and parallel to the right ribbons. Now there should be three ribbons on the right and one on the left.

3. Fold the outer right ribbon under the adjacent ribbon and over the next. Pin. Now there should be two ribbons on each side.

4. Continue braiding in this pattern to the desired length. Stitch the ribbon lengths at each end to secure. Carefully iron braid flat. To make a length of braid longer than the board, braid to the end of the board. Secure beginning ends. Unpin and move the completed trim up the board. Repin at the top and continue braiding.

FIVE-PLY BRAID

This trim can also be braided with one, two, or five colors.

Instructions

1. Pin the ends of the ribbon lengths side-by-side to the board. Starting with the right outside ribbon, weave it over to the left, going under the adjacent ribbon, over the next, under the next and over the last.

2. Repeat this weaving pattern with the ribbon that has shifted to the outside right.

3. Continue in this pattern, pinning the ribbons to keep them right-side up and relatively flat.

4. Stitch the ribbon lengths at each end to secure. To make a length of braid longer than the board, braid to the end of the board. Secure beginning ends. Unpin and move the completed trim up the board. Repin at the top and continue braiding. This braid is flexible and can be applied to curved edges.

RIBBONS AND SUPPLIES

ribbon, 1/8" (3 mm) wide in one, two, or five colors, each cut to a length of 1¼ times the desired length of the finished trim

pins

pinable surface, such as an ironing board or piece of foam core

needle and thread

FOUR-STRAND BOX STITCH BRAID

RIBBONS AND SUPPLIES

grosgrain ribbon, ⅛" to ¼" (3 mm to 6 mm) wide in one or two colors. One yard (0.92 m) of each ribbon will yield about 2" (5 cm) of finished braid.

needle and thread or fabric glue

This braid can be made with one or two colors of ribbon.

Instructions

1. Overlap the centers of the ribbons, making one length vertical and the other horizontal.

2. Working with the vertical ribbon and keeping the ends parallel, bring the top end of the ribbon down and the lower end of the ribbon up.

3. Weave the right horizontal ribbon over to the left, crossing over the right vertical ribbon and under the left vertical ribbon. Weave the left horizontal ribbon over to the right, crossing over the left vertical ribbon and under the right vertical ribbon.

4. Pull the ribbons ends to create a woven square.

5. Repeat step 2, bringing the top vertical ribbon down and the lower vertical ribbon up.

6. Weave the left horizontal ribbon over and under the vertical ribbons. Weave the right horizontal ribbon over and under the vertical ribbons. Pull ribbon ends to create a woven square.

7. One complete turn has been woven. Continue to follow steps 2 to 6 to weave the desired length of braid. Sew small stitches or add drops of glue to the ribbon to hold the last turn of braiding in place. Trim excess ribbon.

> **TIP**
> Add hardware for a key chain or zipper pull to the center of the ribbon before the braiding starts.

SIX-STRAND BOX STITCH BRAID

RIBBONS AND SUPPLIES

grosgrain ribbon, ⅛" to ¼" (3 mm to 6 mm) wide in one or three colors. One yard (0.92 m) of two ribbons and two yards (1.85 m) of the third ribbon will yield about 2" (5 cm) of finished braid.

needle and thread or fabric glue

This braid can be made with one or three colors of ribbon.

Instructions

1. Place the centers of the shorter ribbons onto the center of the longer ribbon. The shorter ribbons should be horizontal and the longer ribbon vertical.

2. Working with the vertical ribbon and keeping the ends parallel, bring the top end of the ribbon down and the lower end of the ribbon up.

3. Weave the top right horizontal ribbon over to the left, crossing over the right vertical ribbon and under the left vertical ribbon. Weave the second horizontal ribbon over to the right, crossing over the left vertical ribbon and under the right vertical ribbon.

4. Following the same pattern, weave the remaining two horizontal ribbons across the vertical ribbons. Pull the ribbons to create a woven rectangle.

5. Repeat step 2, bringing the top vertical ribbon down and the lower vertical ribbon up.

6. Weave the top left horizontal ribbon over to the right, crossing over the left vertical ribbon and under the right vertical ribbon. Weave the second horizontal ribbon over to the left, crossing over the right vertical ribbon and under left vertical ribbon.

7. Following the same pattern, weave across the last two horizontal rows. Pull ribbons to create a woven rectangle.

8. One complete turn has been woven. Continue to follow steps 2 to 7 to weave the desired length of braid. Sew small stitches or add drops of glue to the ribbon to hold the last turn of braiding in place. Trim excess ribbon.

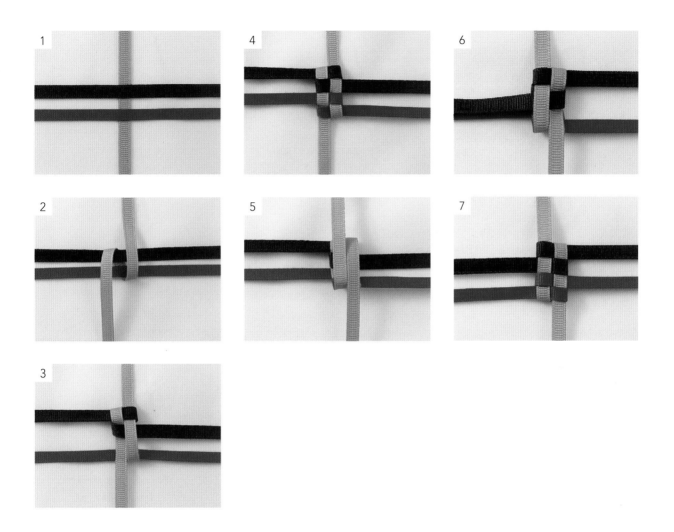

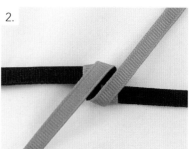

RIBBONS AND SUPPLIES

grosgrain ribbon, ⅛" to ¼" (3 mm to 6 mm) wide in one or two colors. One yard (0.92 m) of each ribbon will yield about 2" (5 cm) of finished braid.

needle and thread or fabric glue

Instructions

1. Follow steps 1 to 4 on page 56 for starting the Four-Strand Box Stitch Braid.

2. Instead of weaving the ribbons straight and parallel, bring the top vertical ribbon down and across to the lower left of the woven square. Bring the lower vertical ribbon up and across to the upper right of the woven square.

3. Weave the right horizontal ribbon across to the upper left, going over the first vertical ribbon and under the next.

4. Weave the left horizontal ribbon across to the lower right, going over the first vertical ribbon and under the next. Pull the ribbon ends to create a woven square. One complete turn has been woven.

5. Rotate the woven square a little so that the ribbons are horizontal and vertical again.

6. Continue to follow steps 2 to 5 to weave the desired length of finished braid. The two colors will spiral around the braid. Sew small stitches or add drops of glue to the ribbon to hold the last turn of braiding in place. Trim excess ribbon.

> ### TIP
> Hardware for a key chain or zipper pull can be added to the center of the ribbon before the braiding starts.

FRINGED RIBBON

The weave structure of grosgrain or petersham ribbon allows for the lengthwise rows to be unraveled to create a fringed ribbon.

Instructions

1. Cut the ribbon to the desired length, based upon the intended use of the fringed ribbon. Carefully cut away one of the selvage edges. Cut straight and as close as possible to the edge.

2. Starting at one end of the ribbon, begin to remove the lengthwise rows of thread. Work in small sections, holding the ribbon taut between two fingers as you move along the length of the ribbon. A needle or pin is helpful for getting the rows started. Pull the threads away from the ribbon. If you're careful, you can unravel several rows of thread at one time.

3. When the fringe is unraveled to the desired depth, seal the ends of the ribbon with nail polish or Fray Check to prevent further raveling.

RIBBONS AND SUPPLIES

grosgrain or petersham ribbon, any width

needle or pin

clear nail polish or Fray Check

TIP

Fringed ribbons can be used to make many embellishments. They can be gathered into a rosette, rolled into a spiral and used as the center of a flower, or sewn into the seam of a pillow.

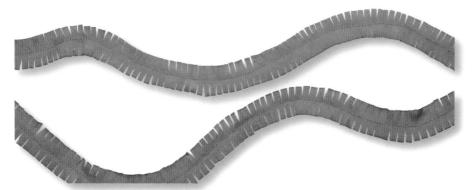

1

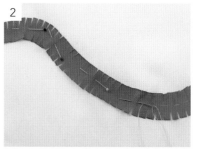

2

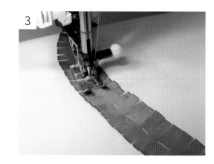

3

RIBBONS AND SUPPLIES

soft taffeta or satin ribbon, ¾" to 1" (2 cm to 2.5 cm) wide. The amount of ribbon needed will depend upon the shape and size of the intended design.

small sharp scissors

Bias silk ribbon is particularly nice for this fringe as the bias cut allows the trim to be easily stretched and eased around curves and formed into decorative shapes.

Instructions

1. Lay the ribbon on a flat working surface. Along both selvage edges, make short cuts toward the center of the ribbon. Make sure to leave a solid section down the center of the ribbon. Make the cuts approximately the same length and distance apart. The sample shown is 1" (2.5 cm) ribbon and the cuts are about ⅜" (1 cm) long and ¼" (6 mm) apart.

2. Arrange the cut ribbon fringe on your project, following a chosen design or curving the ribbon in a freeform shape. Baste the ribbon to your project with running stitches. Ease the ribbon into the desired shape as you sew it in place.

3. Machine-stitch the ribbon to your project, sewing along the center of the ribbon with either straight or decorative stitches. Remove the basting thread.

TIP

If the fringe is used on a project that will be laundered or receive a lot of wear, the cut ribbon may fray. That adds to the look of the cut-work trim. For less fraying, select a bias-cut ribbon.

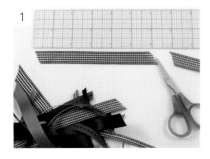

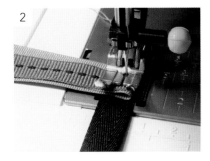

Choose ribbons in a range of colors or mix bits and pieces of ribbons leftover from other projects.

Instructions

1. Determine how wide you want the fringe to be and cut the various ribbons two times that length. The fringe shown is 3" (7.5 cm). The ribbons are cut 6" (15 cm) long. Cut the ends diagonally to prevent fraying.

2. Place twill tape under the presser foot of sewing machine and sew a few stitches. Randomly select two or three ribbon lengths and hold them as a group. Fold the group in half. Place the fold on the edge of the twill tape and begin sewing down the twill tape ¼" (6 mm) from the edge. Use the presser foot as a guide.

3. Continue to sew folded groups to the twill tape, aligning each group against the next so there are no spaces between the groups. Make the fringe as long as desired.

RIBBONS AND SUPPLIES

ribbons, any width, type, or color. The amount of ribbon needed will depend upon the desired width of the fringe and the types of ribbon selected.

ruler

½" (1.3 cm) twill tape

sewing machine and thread

TIP

• To sew fringe inside a seam, fold along the stitching line and press up.

• To apply fringe to a surface, cover the stitching line with another trim.

• Add other trims, rick rack, or yarn into the fringe.

• Looped fringe can be made by keeping the groups of ribbons folded and sewing the ends of the ribbons to the twill tape.

LOOPY FRINGE

RIBBONS AND SUPPLIES

soft ribbons, ⅛" to 1" (3 mm to 2.5 cm) wide. The exact amount needed will depend upon the width of the selected ribbons and the desired width and length of the finished trim.

hairpin lace loom

adhseive tape

½" (1.3 cm) twill tape the desired length of the finished fringe

sewing machine and thread

This fringe can be made with just one color or type of ribbon or can be made with a variety of ribbons. For best results, select soft ribbons, such as satins or hand-dyed silks.

Instructions

1. Adjust bars on the hairpin lace loom for twice the desired finished width of the trim. The tubes on the loom shown are set to 4" (10 cm) and will make a 2" (5 cm) loopy fringe. Holding one or two ribbons together, tape the ends to the cross bar on one end of the loom. Wind the ribbons around the tubes, keeping the ribbons flat and overlapping at each pass by about ¼" (6 mm) so there are no gaps.

2. Tape the ribbons to the opposite cross bar but do not cut, unless you want to make a fringe that is only the length of the loom. Center the twill tape over the wrapped ribbon and tape the end to the beginning cross bar.

3. Position the loom under the presser foot of the sewing machine, centering the twill tape under the needle. Sew a line of stitches down the center of the twill tape.

4. When you have stitched as far as possible to the end of the loom, secure stitches. Remove tape holding ribbons and twill tape. Remove the beginning cross bar and slide up the sewn fringe, leaving a few loops on each tube. Replace cross bar and continue wrapping ribbons around the loom. Tape ribbons to hold temporarily. Reposition twill tape at the center of the wrapped loops. Staring at the point where the stitching ended, continue to sew a line of stitching down the center of the twill tape. Repeat until the loopy fringe is the desired length.

5. Trim ribbon ends to about ¼" (6 mm) from the center stitching. Fold ribbon loops in half. Fold twill tape in half and press to create the header for the fringe. Insert the header between seams when sewing the fringe to a project or cover it with a decorative trim.

1

3

5

2

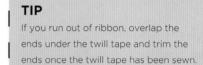

4

TIP

If you run out of ribbon, overlap the
ends under the twill tape and trim the
ends once the twill tape has been sewn.

Rosettes and Leaves

Gathered, pleated, and folded rosettes and leaves have been popular ribbon embellishments throughout history. Victorian ladies often created them to decorate their clothing, accessories, and their homes. Handbooks from that era give instructions for making ribbon "fancies" to add to a frock, hat, or a special gift.

Circles of ribbon, called cockades, were designed to identify rank among military personnel. These ornaments evolved to be quite elaborate and became symbolic of allegiance to political associations.

Today we use a simple looped ribbon to associate ourselves with various social causes, such as the pink ribbon loop that symbolizes support for breast cancer. Other colors of looped ribbon are associated with various organizations or social movements. And, of course, one of the most universal and coveted ribbon designs is a round, pleated circle of blue ribbon, awarded to acknowledge a first-place finish in any type of race or contest.

These types of embellishments, fashioned with ribbons readily available today, can still be used for personal adornment or home décor accents; sew one to a clutch bag, make several to use as a set of napkin rings, add them on gift packaging instead of the usual bow, or commemorate a special occasion or person with a not-necessarily blue ribbon. Use these instructions as a starting point. Try different ribbon sizes and combine several types of rosettes to make a layered cockade. Make it yours and it will be special.

PULLED WIRE ROSE

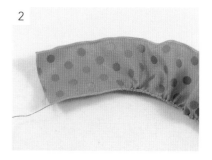

RIBBONS AND SUPPLIES

wire-edge ribbon: 1 yd (0.92 m) of ⅞" (2.2 cm) ribbon will make a 3" (7.5 cm) rose; 1½ to 2 yd (1.4 to 1.85 m) of 1½" (4 cm) ribbon will make a 4" (10 cm) rose.

needle and thread

pins

Stripe, plaid, and dot ribbons make whimsical roses. Solid and ombre shaded ribbons make more realistic roses.

Instructions

1. Tie an overhand knot at one end of the ribbon.

2. At the other end of the ribbon, gently pull one of the wires. Carefully ease the ribbon along the wire to gather it to half its original length. The edge that is gathered will be the inner part of the rose.

3. Pull out 1" (2.5 cm) of wire from the ungathered side of the ribbon. Twist the two wires together close to the ribbon and securely hold the gathers. Trim the long wire, leaving about 1" (2.5 cm).

4. Just above the knot, roll the ribbon tightly to form the center of the rose. Double thread the needle and secure the center with a few stitches. Do not cut the thread.

5. Continue to roll and loosely coil the ribbon around the center. Keep the knot exposed and do not allow the gathered ribbon selvages to overlap. The edges should spiral out from the center. Pin as you wrap. Loosely stitch the layers in place. Fold the ribbon end to the back of the rose and secure with a few stitches. Trim thread and excess wire. Manipulate and shape the outer edges of the rose.

3

4

5

TIPS

1. To make a vintage rose variation, use 2 yds (1.85 m) of 1½" (4 cm) wire-edge ribbon. Follow steps 1 to 3 above. Gather the ribbon to 1 yard (0.92 m). Place the gathered ribbon in cold water. Remove excess water and lay on flat surface. Starting at the knot, tightly pleat and scrunch the ribbon down the length.

2. Squeeze excess water out into a towel and gently open the ball of ribbon, leaving the wrinkles in place. The ribbon length will be about 18" (45.5 cm). Allow to dry. Carefully press the wrinkles flat with an iron. Gently straighten out the gathered edge of the ribbon to a length of one yard (0.92 m). Do not straighten out the wrinkles along the ungathered edge.

3. Follow steps 4 to 6 above to complete the vintage rose. Do not over-manipulate the outer petals. They should be wrinkled to achieve the vintage look.

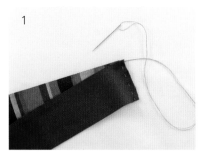

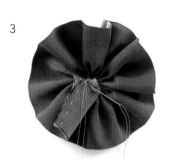

RIBBONS AND SUPPLIES

ribbon: 9" to 12" (23 cm to 30.4 cm) of ⅞" (2.2 cm) ribbon will make a 2" (5 cm) rosette; 15" to 18" (38 cm to 45.5 cm) of 1½" (4 cm) ribbon will make a 3¼" (8.5 cm) rosette

thread to match ribbon

needle

Instructions

1. Fold ribbon, right sides together, to form a circle. With double threaded needle, sew cut ends together with a ⅛" (3 mm) seam allowance. Secure thread at the end but do not cut.

2. Sew running stitching close to one edge of the ribbon.

3. Pull up stitches to gather the rosette tightly in the center. Knot thread and cut excess.

TIP

Make a double gathered rosette by sewing a smaller rosette onto a larger rosette. Sew a button to the center.

FIGURE EIGHT DOUBLE ROSETTE

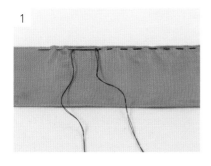

Instructions

1. Fold ribbon in half and mark center points on each side of the ribbon. With thread doubled in needle, start at the middle point and sew running stitches along one edge of the ribbon out to the end.

2. Pull thread to gather ribbon. Stitch the end of gathered edge to the midpoint and form ribbon into a circle. Knot thread and trim excess.

3. Start at the middle point on the opposite side of the ribbon and sew running stitches along the edge out to the end.

4. Pull thread to gather ribbon. Sew the end of the gathered edge to the midpoint and form the ribbon into a second circle. Backstitch to secure thread. Slipstitch raw edges of ribbon together at the back of the rosette. If desired, sew buttons onto the centers of the two rosettes.

RIBBONS AND SUPPLIES

taffeta ribbon: 18" (45.5 cm) of ⅞" (2.2 cm) ribbon will make a 2" x 3" (5 cm x 7.5 cm) rosette. 24" (61 cm) of 1½" (4 cm) ribbon will make a 3" x 4½" (7.5 cm x 11.5 cm) rosette. If the selected ribbon has a wired edge, pull out both wires. If using a variegated ribbon, each half of the rosette will be a different color.

needle and thread

fabric marking pen

2 buttons (optional)

CONTINUOUS PETAL ROSETTE

RIBBONS AND SUPPLIES

ribbon that gathers easily: 24" (61 cm) of 1½" (4 cm) ribbon will make a 3" (7.5 cm) rosette. 18" (45.5 cm) of 1" (2.5 cm) ribbon will make a 2" (5 cm) rosette. Both colors will show if a double-sided ribbon is used.

needle and thread

ruler and fabric marking pen

Instructions

1. Starting ½" (1.3 cm) from the end, place six marks along one edge of the ribbon. For a 1½" (4 cm) ribbon, make the marks 3½" (9 cm) apart. For a 1" (2.5 cm) ribbon, make the marks 2" (5 cm) apart. Trim excess ribbon ½" (1.3 cm) beyond last mark and set aside.

2. With thread doubled in needle, stitch running stitches along the marked edge of the ribbon. At each mark, sew stitches straight up to the opposite edge of the ribbon and back down.

3. As you sew, pull the stitches tightly to gather and form five petals. Gently shape and cup petals. Stitch the last petal to the first petal to form a circle.

4. Tie an overhand knot at the center of the excess ribbon. Bring the ends together and push them through the center of the rosette. Secure with a few stitches and trim ribbon ends.

TIP

For a double rosette, sew a small rosette on top of a large rosette before adding the center.

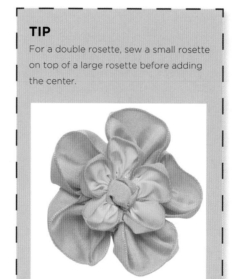

1

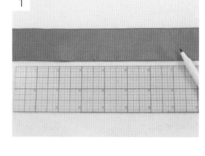

2

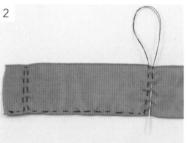

3

4

RUCHED ROSETTE

Instructions

1. Following the instructions for Serpentine Ruching on page 13, make a ruched trim 14" (35.5 cm) long.

2. Stitch one end of the ruched trim to the center of the buckram circle.

3. Spiral the trim around the center point, tucking the petals around and underneath each other. Continue to stitch the ruched trim onto the buckram circle.

4. When you've run out of trim, tuck under the tail of the trim and stitch the edge of the buckram circle to the outer petals.

RIBBONS AND SUPPLIES

ribbon that gathers easily: 1½ yd (1.3 m) of ⅞" to 1" (2.2cm to 2.5cm) ribbon will make a 3" (7.5 cm) rosette.

needle and thread

2¼" (5.5 cm) circle of buckram

PULLED THREAD ROSETTE

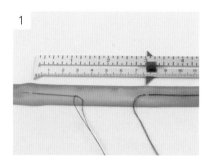

1

Instructions

1. With thread doubled in needle, sew a small stitch into the ribbon, about 1" (2.5 cm) from the end. Begin sewing long running stitches down the ribbon, catching just a few threads. Space the stitches 2" (5 cm) apart on the ¼" (6 mm) ribbon and 3" (7.5 cm) apart on the ½" (1.3 cm) ribbon.

2. After several stitches, pull the thread to gather the ribbon into loops. Continue to stitch running stitches and gather up the ribbon down its length.

3. Stop stitching about 1" (22.5 cm) from the end of the ribbon. Gather the loops tightly and secure the thread at the center of the rosette.

2

RIBBONS AND SUPPLIES

soft ribbon, such as taffeta or silk satin: 2 yd (1.85 m) of ¼" (6 mm) ribbon will make a 2" (5 cm) rosette. 3 yd (2.7 m) of ½" (1.3 cm) ribbon will make a 3" (7.5 cm) rosette.

needle and thread

ruler

3

TIPS

Sew two ribbons together for a layered effect. Place the narrow ribbon on top of the wider ribbon. To keep the narrow ribbon on top, sew the long running stitches along the back of the wider ribbon, catching the narrow ribbon with the stitches. To flatten the loops, sew a button at the center of the rosette.

WHEEL ROSETTE

1

2

3

Instructions

1. Cut twelve 3" (7.5 cm) lengths of ribbon. If you are using two colors, cut six lengths of each color. Fold each ribbon length in half and slipstitch raw edges together or secure with a drop of fabric glue.

2. Position and sew or glue the loops around the circle base, each overlapping the previous one. If you are using two colors, alternate them around the circle.

3. Make sure to overlap the loops evenly; tuck the final loop under the first one.

4. Sew one or two buttons to the center of the rosette.

RIBBONS AND SUPPLIES

ribbon: 1 yd (.9 m) of ⅞" (2.2 cm) wide. If using two ribbons as shown in sample, you will need 18" (45.5 cm) of each. The finished rosette will be 3½" (9 cm)

1¾" (4.5 cm) circle of buckram or felt

needle and thread

fabric glue (optional)

one or two buttons

CROSS ROSETTE

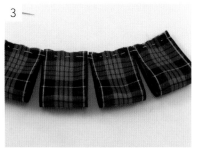

RIBBONS AND SUPPLIES

ribbon: 10" (25.5 cm) of ⅞" (2.2 cm) ribbon will make a 2½" (6.5 cm) rosette; 16" (40.5 cm) of 1½" (4 cm) ribbon will make a 3½" (9 cm) rosette

thread to match ribbon

needle

button

Instructions

1. Cut four 2½" (6.5 cm) lengths of ⅞" (2.2 cm) ribbon or four 4" (10 cm) lengths of 1½" (4 cm) ribbon. If the ribbon is a plaid or check, cut the lengths at the same point in the pattern so each loop will be the same.

2. Form the first loop by folding one ribbon length in half, matching raw edges. With thread doubled in needle, sew close to the edges using running stitch. Do not knot or cut thread.

3. In the same way, form three more loops and sew stitches close to the edges, placing the loops side-by-side onto the thread.

4. Pull up thread to gather loops together in the center. Attach the last loop to the first loop to form the rosette. Sew a button to the center of the rosette. Secure thread and trim excess.

LOOPY ROSETTE

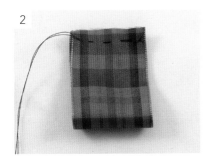

Instructions

1. Cut six 3½" (9 cm) lengths of ⅞" (2.2 cm) ribbon or six 4" (10 cm) lengths of 1½" (4 cm) ribbon. If the ribbon is a plaid or check, cut the lengths at the same point in the pattern so each loop will be the same.

2. Form the first loop by folding one ribbon length in half, matching raw edges. With thread doubled in needle, sew running stitches close to the edges. Do not knot or cut thread.

3. In the same way, form five more loops and sew stitches close to the edges, placing the loops side by side onto the thread.

4. Pull up thread to gather loops together in the center. Attach the last loop to the first loop to form the rosette.

5. Sew a button to the center of the rosette. Secure thread and trim excess.

RIBBONS AND SUPPLIES

ribbon: 21" (53.5 cm) of ⅞" (2.2 cm) ribbon will make a 3" (7.5 cm) rosette; 24" (61 cm) of 1½" (4 cm) ribbon will make a 3½" (9 cm) rosette

thread to match ribbon

needle

button

TWISTED PETAL ROSETTE

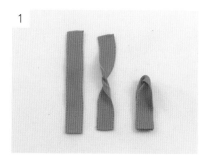

RIBBONS AND SUPPLIES

ribbon: 30" (76 cm) of ⅜" (1 cm)
ribbon will make a 2½" (6.5 cm)
rosette.

needle and thread

button

TIP

To make leaves, cut a 3" (7.5
cm) length of ribbon for each
leaf. Twist it in the center and
fold in half, as done for the
rosette petals. Sew the leaves
to the back of the rosette.

---

*Consider using double-sided satin or velvet ribbons
for this project. These ribbons are particularly
attractive as both sides will show and add
dimension to the finished rosette*

Instructions

1. Cut twelve 2½" (6.5 cm) lengths of ribbon. Tightly
twist each ribbon length at the center and fold in
half.

2. As each ribbon is twisted and folded, insert a
threaded needle into the petal and make a stitch.
Do not cut thread. Continue to add all twelve
petals.

3. Once all the petals have been placed onto the
thread, pull up to gather the petals and form the
rosette. Sew a button to the center.

FOLDED PETAL ROSETTE

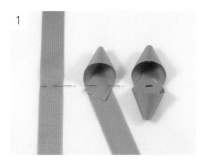

Instructions

1. Cut two 7" (18 cm) lengths of ribbon for the inner petals and two 8" (20.5 cm) lengths of ribbon for the outer petals. Mark the center of the ribbon lengths with a pin. To form each length into a set of petals, fold one end to the right and to the back. Overlap the end at the center of the ribbon. Pin. Fold the other end to the left and to the back. Overlap the end at the center, aligning with the other end of the ribbon. The ribbon will form a figure 8 shape. Pin at the center. Stitch to hold.

2. Center and sew one set of inner petals onto the second set of inner petals. Center and sew one set of outer petals onto the second set of outer petals.

3. Center and sew the inner petals to the outer petals, making sure that the outer petals alternate with the inner petals to form a balanced rosette.

4. Cut an 8" (20.5 cm) length of ribbon for the center. With thread doubled in needle, sew running stitches down the center of the length of the ribbon. Pull thread tightly to gather ribbon into a ball. Knot thread to hold gathers but do not cut

5. Sew the center to the middle of the rosette. If you want to add tails onto the rosette, fold the remaining ribbon in half, slightly angling the ends. Cut ends of ribbon into a V. Stitch folded tails to the back of rosette.

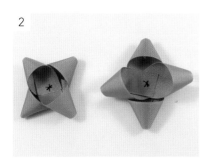

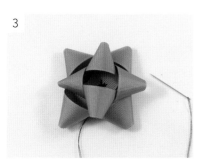

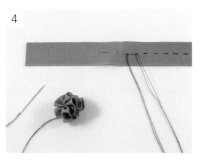

RIBBONS AND SUPPLIES

grosgrain ribbon: 1⅓ yd (122 cm) of ⅞" (2.2 cm) will make a 3" (7.6 cm) rosette with 4" (10 cm) tails

needle and thread

pins

1

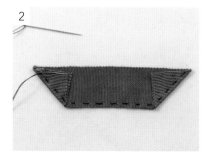

2

3

4

RIBBONS AND SUPPLIES

ribbon, ⅝" to 1½" (1.5 cm to 4 cm) wide, cut to 6 to 10 times the width of the ribbon, depending upon the desired size of the finished leaf

needle and thread

pins

Instructions

1. Fold the ribbon in half, crosswise. Fold the ends up diagonally, to rest just below the upper edge, forming a boat shape. Pin ends in place.

2. With thread doubled in needle, sew using running stitch down one diagonal fold, across the bottom of the boat and up the opposite diagonal fold.

3. Pull stitches to gather to desired fullness. Knot and cut excess thread.

4. Open leaf and adjust gathers.

HOUSE LEAF

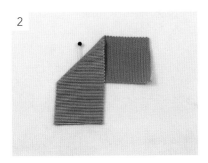

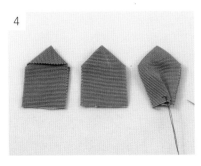

Instructions

1. Place a pin at the center point of the ribbon.

2. Fold the left end of the ribbon down on the diagonal, making sure the midpoint pin is at the center of the fold. Press.

3. Fold the right end of the ribbon down on the diagonal, making sure the midpoint pin is at the top of the triangle formed. Press.

4. The folded ribbon will look like a small house. One side has a roof line. The other side is plain. Work from the plain side and fold a small pleat at the bottom of the house to shape the leaf. Secure with a few stitches.

RIBBONS AND SUPPLIES

⅞" (2.2 cm) or wider ribbon,
cut 2½ times the width of the ribbon

pins

iron

needle and thread

PRAIRIE POINT LEAF

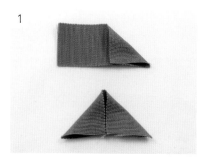

1

2

RIBBONS AND SUPPLIES

ribbon that gathers easily, 2½"
(6.5 cm) of 1" (2.5 cm) wide or 3"
(7.5 cm) of 1½" (4 cm) wide

needle and thread

Instructions

1. Fold the ribbon in half and press along the fold
with your finger to mark the center. Fold each end
of the ribbon down to the center line, forming a
triangle.

2. With thread doubled in needle, sew a line of
running stitches across the bottom of the folded ribbon. Gather stitches to form leaf. Secure thread and
trim excess. Either side of the leaf can be placed
facing upward.

TIPS
- If you have selected a wire-
edge ribbon, remove wires
before making leaves.
- Variegated ribbons make
beautiful prairie point leaves.
Alternate the placement of the
colors along the center line.
- Consider making leaves from
stripes and checks and other
fun patterns. All leaves are not
green.

PRAIRIE POINT ROSETTE

Instructions

1. Cut sixteen 3" (7.5 cm) lengths of ribbon. Follow the instructions for making a Prairie Point Leaf opposite. Make 16 prairie point leaves for the rosette petals.

2. Pin four petals evenly around the buckram circle. Position them so that the tips of the petals are 1" (2.5 cm) beyond the edge of the circle. Sew each petal to the circle.

3. Pin and sew four petals around the circle, positioning them between the first four petals. This will complete the outside ring of petals.

4. For the inner ring of petals, evenly pin four petals to the circle. They should be positioned between the outer petals and the tips should be ½" (1.3 cm) lower. Sew the petals to the circle.

5. Pin and sew the remaining four petals around the circle, positioning them between the first four petals of the inner ring. Sew the button to the center of the rosette.

RIBBONS AND SUPPLIES

ribbon that gathers easily: 1⅓ yd (122 cm) of 1½" (4 cm) ribbon will make a 4" (10 cm) rosette. If the ribbon is wire-edged, remove both wires.

needle and thread

pins

2¼" (5.5 cm) buckram circle

button

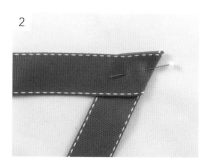

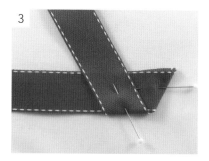

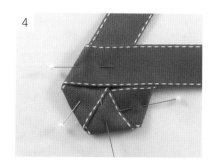

RIBBONS AND SUPPLIES

ribbon: ½ yd (0.5 m) of ⅞" (23 mm)
ribbon will make a 2" (5 cm) button

needle and thread

pins

one or two buttons

For this rosette select a ribbon that is the same on both sides, as each will show when folded. Striped ribbons add interest to the lines of the folds.

Instructions

1. Fold ribbon at a 60-degree angle at the center.

2. Fold the right-hand ribbon over the left and pin.

3. Bring the right ribbon over the left, aligning fold with inner edge of left ribbon. Pin.

4. Repeat this folding pattern two more times. To assure that the button is symmetrical, make sure the inner edge of the ribbon is parallel to the edge of the first fold.

5. Repeat folding pattern two more times. Slip ribbon tails under the first point.

6. Trim excess ribbon and handstitch layers at the back to secure. Sew one or two buttons to the center of the rosette.

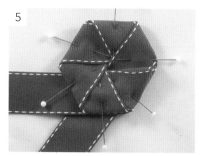

FOLDED PETAL LEAVES

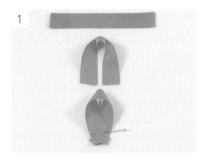

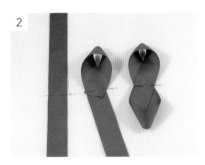

TIPS

• The leaves can be ironed to flatten them before they are attached to the rosette.
• The leaves can be positioned with the points cupping up or down.

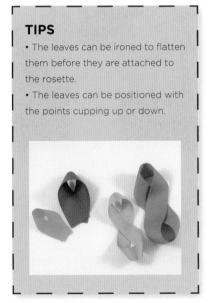

Instructions

1. To make a single leaf, fold the ends of the ribbon length to the back. Overlap the ends and pin. Stitch or glue to hold.

2. To make double leaves, mark the center of the ribbon length with a pin. Fold one end to the right and to the back. Overlap the end at the center of the ribbon. Pin. Fold the other end to left and to the back. Overlap the end at the center, aligning with the other end of the ribbon. The ribbon will form a figure 8 shape. Pin at the center. Stitch or glue to hold.

RIBBONS AND SUPPLIES

ribbon: 4" to 5" (10 cm to 12.5 cm) of ⅝" or ⅞" (1.5 cm or 2.2 cm) for a single leaf; 8" to 12" (20.5 cm to 30.5 cm) of ⅝" or ⅞" (1.5 cm or 2.2 cm) for double leaves. The exact ribbon length will depend upon how long you want the finished leaves to be in proportion to the rosette you are embellishing.

needle and thread or fabric glue

pins

Instructions

1. Following instructions on page 22 for making Knife Pleat Trim, pleat the outer pleat ribbon. Make the pleats ¾" (2 cm) deep. As each pleat is folded, angle and pin in the edge so that the trim curves and forms a semicircle about 3 ½" (9 cm) wide on the inside edge. Baste along the edge to hold the pleats. Turn back both raw edges of the ribbon and slipstitch to secure. Pin and slipstitch the pleats to the buckram semicircle.

2. Use the same technique to pleat the inner pleat ribbon. Angle the pleats a little more than the outer pleats so that the trim curves and forms a semicircle about 2 ½" (6.5 cm) on the inside edge. Baste. Slipstitch ends. Pin and slipstitch the inner pleats to the buckram semicircle, covering the sewn edge of the outer pleats.

3. Cut seven 3" (7.5 cm) lengths of ⅞" (2.2 cm) ribbon for the inner loops. Fold each length in half and pin. Working from left to right, pin and stitch the inner loops around the semicircle, covering the sewn edge of the inner pleats.

4. Cut four 2 ½" (6.5 cm) lengths of ⅞" (2.2 cm) ribbon for the center loops. Fold each length in half. Pin and sew the center loops around the semicircle, covering the sewn edges of the inner loops.

5. Overlap the ends of the remaining ⅞" (2.2 cm) ribbon, making a center loop with streamers. Secure loop with a few stitches. Trim streamer ends on the diagonal. Sew the loop and streamers to the center of the semicircle, covering the sewn edges of the center loops.

RIBBONS AND SUPPLIES

⅞ yd (80 cm) of 1½" (4 cm) ribbon for outer pleats

¾ yd (68.5 cm) of 1½" (4 cm) ribbon for inner pleats

21" (53.5 cm) of ⅞" (2.2 cm) ribbon for inner loops

½ yd (45.5 cm) of ⅞" (2.2 cm) ribbon for center loops and streamers

5" (12.5 cm) diameter semicircle of buckram

finished size: 6½" (16.5 cm) wide x 6¼" (16 cm) long

1

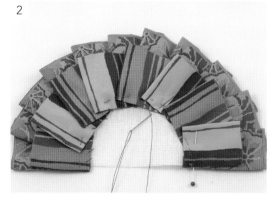

2

3

4

5

OCTAGONAL ROSETTE

For this rosette, select a ribbon that is the same on both sides, as each side will show when the rosette is formed.

Instructions

1. Cut a 12½" (31.5 cm) length of ribbon. Fold the length in half and hand or machine stitch the ends together with a ¼" (6 mm) seam allowance to form a circle. Press seam open. Use a pin to mark the fold line for the center of the ribbon length. Refold the circle, matching the seam line with the fold line. Mark the new fold lines with a pin, evenly dividing the ribbon circle into fourths.

2. Use a ruler and pencil to mark horizontal and vertical center lines on the buckram square. With the raw edges of the seam against the buckram square, align the seam line and the three pins with the center lines. Flatten ribbon to form an octagon shape. Slipstitch the inside of the ribbon octagon to the buckram square.

3. Cut a 10½" (26.5 cm) length of ribbon. Follow steps 1 and 2 again to make the next inner ribbon circle. Sew it to the buckram square. Make sure that the seam lines align at the bottom of the rosette.

4. Cut an 8½" (21.5 cm) length of ribbon and a 6½" (16.5 cm) length of ribbon for the next two inner ribbon circles. Follow steps 1 and 2 again to form and sew the next two inner circles to the buckram. All seam lines should align at the bottom of the rosette.

5. Fold the remaining length of ribbon in half, angling the ends slightly to form streamers. Slipstitch the fold line to the center of the buckram so that the streamers cover the seam lines. Cut the ends of the ribbon on the diagonal. Sew the button to the center of the rosette.

RIBBONS AND SUPPLIES

ribbon: 1⅓ yd (122 cm) of ⅞" to 1" (2.2 cm to 2.5 cm) wide

2¾" (7 cm) square of buckram

large button

pins

needle and thread

pencil and ruler

sewing machine (optional)

finished size: 4" (9.7 cm) wide x 6½" (17 cm) long

1

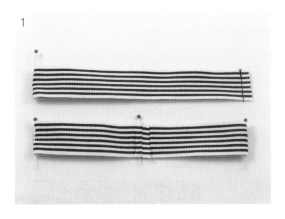

2

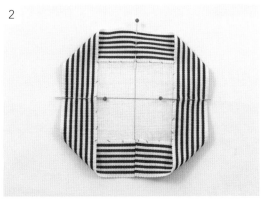

3

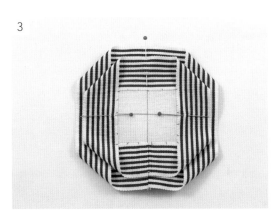

4

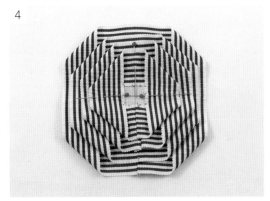

5

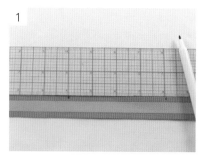

1

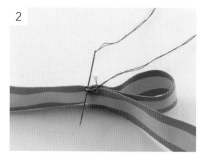

2

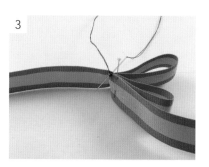

3

4

RIBBONS AND SUPPLIES

ribbon, with enough body to hold a soft crease: 1½ yd (137 cm) of ⅞" (2.2 cm) ribbon will make a 4" (10 cm) medallion; 1⅛ yd (102.8 cm) of ⅝" (1.5 cm) ribbon will make a 3" (7.5 cm) medallion

ruler and fabric marking pen

needle and thread

pins

pinable surface, such as an ironing board or piece of foam core

iron

circle of buckram: 2½" (6.5 cm) for ⅞" (2.2 cm) ribbon, 1¾" (4.5 cm) for ⅝" (1.5 cm) ribbon

button

The wrong side of the ribbon will show at the center of the medallion. If you use a two-sided ribbon, one color will be on the outer edge and the other color at the center. Striped ribbons show off the spiraling folded pattern.

5

Instructions

1. Place small marks along one selvage edge of the ribbon to create the spacing for the loops. The spaces should be a little more than four times the width of the ribbon. For the medallions shown, the marks are 4" (10 cm) apart on the ⅞" (2.2 cm) ribbon and 3" (7.5 cm) apart on the ⅝" (1.5 cm) ribbon.

2. Fold the ribbon back onto itself at the second mark. Place the second mark on top of the first to create the first loop. Pin to hold. With thread doubled in needle, sew a few stitches at the folded edge point to hold the loop together. Do not knot or cut the thread. Let the threaded needle hang.

3. Fold the ribbon back onto itself at the third mark. Place the third mark on top of the second mark to create the second loop. Align the edges of the ribbon and repin to hold the second loop in place. Sew a few stitches to connect the second loop to the first at the folded edge points. Let the threaded needle hang.

4. Continue to fold and stitch together eleven loops. Secure thread but do not cut.

5. Place the ribbon ends right side together. Join the loops into a circle and sew with a few stitches at the folded edge points of the ribbon tails. Knot thread securely and trim.

6. Turn medallion over so stitching is on the back. Place the medallion on a pinable surface. Evenly position and pin the outer loops around the medallion center. A pattern of loops will appear at the center. The ends of the ribbon will fan out as tails. Carefully iron the medallion folds to flatten.

7. To keep the loops in position and add stability, pin the buckram circle to the back of the medallion and slipstitch to the ribbon loops. Sew a button to the center of the medallion. Trim the ribbon tails diagonally or into inverted Vs.

6

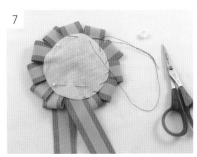

7

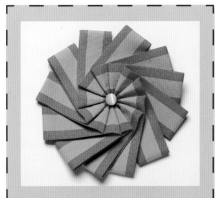

TIP

The medallion can be made without tails.

1. Before sewing on the buckram circle, trim the ribbon tail that is between the last loop and the beginning end of the ribbon to about 1" (2.5 cm).

2. Fold the beginning end of the ribbon back, creating a final twelfth loop. Slipstitch the beginning end of the ribbon to the back of the medallion, encasing the raw edge of the trimmed ribbon tail.

Instructions

1. Following the instructions for Accordion Pleats on page 24, pleat and press the rosette ribbon on the pleater board. When cool, remove the pleated ribbon from the pleater.

2. Fold ribbon, right sides together, trimming ends to align pleat folds. Stitch ends to form a circle. With thread doubled in needle, sew running stitches around the inside of the circle. Pull stitches to tighten the inside of the circle.

3. Fold the center ribbon in half lengthwise. Starting at one end, tightly roll the folded ribbon into a coil. From the folded side of the ribbon, sew the coiled layers together as the center is rolled to the end of the ribbon.

4. With the edges of the ribbon center up, sew the center to the middle of the pleated rosette.

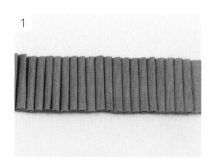

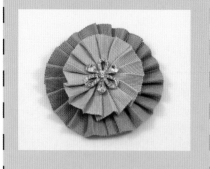

RIBBONS AND SUPPLIES

ribbon, such as petersham, that will hold pleats well when pressed: 12" (30.5 cm) of ⅞" (2.2 cm) ribbon will make a 2¼" (5.5 cm) rosette; 18" (45.5 cm) of 1½" (4 cm) ribbon will make a 3½" (9 cm) rosette.

16" (40.5 cm) of ⅝" (1.5 cm) ribbon for the rosette center

pleater board

thin ruler or credit card

iron

pressing cloth

white vinegar

needle

thread to match ribbon

TIP

To make a double-pleated rosette, make a rosette from ⅞" (2.2 cm) ribbon and one from 1½" (4 cm) ribbon. Sew the smaller rosette onto the center of the larger rosette. Instead of the rolled ribbon center, sew a button to the center.

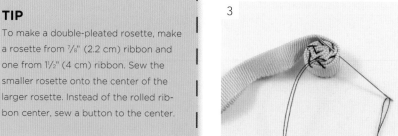

PETAL POINTS COCKADE

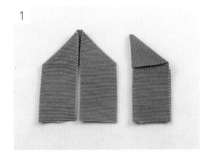

Instructions

1. Cut twelve 5" (12.5 cm) lengths of ⅞" (2.2 cm) ribbon. At the center of each length, fold the ends down, creating a triangle shape. Press. Fold the triangles in half to create the petal points. Press.

2. With all the folds going in the same direction, evenly position the petal points around the buckram circle. The bottom of each folded triangle should be at the edge of the circle. The ends of the ribbons will overlap in the center of the circle. Pin.

3. Turn the circle over and slipstitch the edge of the circle to all the petal points. Secure the overlapping ribbons at the center with more stitches.

4. Following the instructions on page 70, make a Gathered Rosette with the 1½" (4 cm) ribbon. Sew the gathered rosette to the center of the circle. Sew a button to the center of the rosette.

RIBBONS AND SUPPLIES

coordinating ribbons that can be easily folded and gathered: 1⅔ yd (1.66 m) of ⅞" (2.2 cm) ribbon and 18" (45.5 cm) of 1½" (4 cm) ribbon will make a 5" (12.5 cm) cockade

iron

3" (7.5 cm) buckram circle

needle and thread

button

TIP
If the cockade is not going to be attached to a project, a felt circle can be stitched to the back to cover the stitching and add stability.

PETAL COCKADE

TIP

Any combination of coordinated ribbons can be used to make a petal cockade. This 6" (15 cm) cockade was made with 2" (5 cm) ribbon for the center gathered rosette and ⅝" (1.5 cm) and ⅞" (2.2 cm) ribbon for the loops. The overlapped loops are sewn with the points to the back. To determine what size to make the buckram circle, make the gathered rosette first and measure the diameter. Cut the circle ½" (1.3 cm) larger than the gathered rosette.

RIBBONS AND SUPPLIES

ribbon: 9" (23 cm) of ⅞" (2.2 cm) wide, 30" (76 cm) of ⅝" (1.5 cm) wide and 1 yd (.9 m) of ⅜" (1 cm) wide will make a 4" (10 cm) cockade

2½" (6.5 cm) buckram circle

ruler

pins

needle and thread

button

Instructions

1. To create the loops that will go around the outside edge of the cockade, cut twelve 2½" (6.5 cm) lengths of the ⅝" (1.5 cm) ribbon. Fold each ribbon length in half, creating a loop. Evenly position and pin the loops around the edge of the buckram circle. They should extend about ¾" (2 cm) beyond the edge of the circle. Stitch the loops to the buckram circle.

2. To create the second row of loops, cut twelve 3" (7.5 cm) lengths of the ⅜" (1 cm) ribbon. Overlap the ends of each length, creating a petal loop. Evenly position and pin the overlapped looped between the folded loops. They should extend about ½" (1.3 cm) beyond the edge of the circle.

3. Stitch the overlapped loops to the buckram circle.

4. Following the instructions on page 70, make a Gathered Rosette with the ⅞" (2.2 cm) ribbon.

5. Sew the gathered rosette to the center of the buckram circle. Sew the button to the center of the gathered rosette.

1

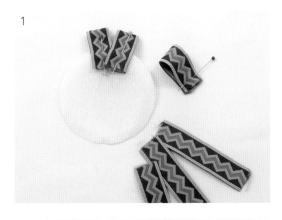

3

2

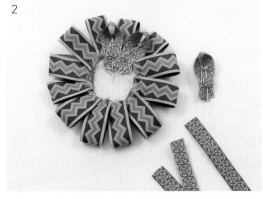

4

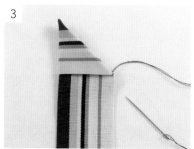

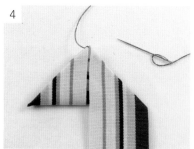

RIBBONS AND SUPPLIES

ribbon with enough body to hold a soft crease: 2½ yd (2.3 m) of 1½" (4 cm) ribbon will make a 5" (12.5 cm) cockade. 1½ yd (1.4 m) of ⅞" (2.2 cm) ribbon will make a 3½" (9 cm) cockade.

needle and thread

clothespins

button (optional)

buckram (optional)

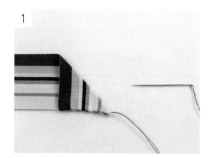

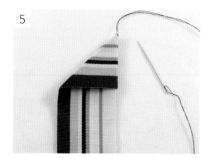

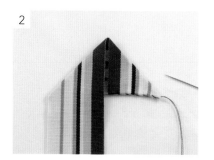

7

8

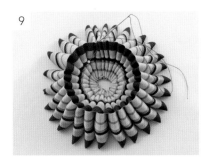

9

10

When selecting ribbon for this cockade, keep in mind that solid colors will show off the folding pattern, while stripes will create an interesting pattern that radiates out from the center of the cockade. Wire-edge ribbons may be used if the wires are removed from both edges.

Instructions

1. Turn under the raw edge ¼" (6 mm) at one end of the ribbon and press. With the wrong side up and the end to the right, fold down the turned back edge of the ribbon to align with the lower selvage edge. With thread doubled in needle, begin at the inside bottom of the triangle just formed and slip-stitch the finished edge to the selvage edge. End stitching at the point of the triangle. Secure thread but do not cut. Leave threaded needle hanging.

2. With the working end of the ribbon to the left, fold the ribbon down to form a large triangle. Leave a small space between the ribbon edges. This gap allows for the next fold of the ribbon.

3. Fold the large triangle in half to the right, with the gap at the inside center. Align the diagonal folds. Insert the threaded needle into the outer tip of the new fold and secure with a stitch. Do not cut thread. Leave needle hanging. One full point has been made.

4. Rotate the upper point of the triangle 90 degrees to the left. Make another triangle by folding the ribbon down and to the left, leaving a small gap between the ribbon edges.

5. Fold the large triangle in half and to the left, with the gap at the inside center. Align the diagonal folds. Insert the threaded needle into the tip of the fold and secure the ribbon with a stitch. Leave the threaded needle hanging.

6. Repeat steps 2 to 5 until you have completed enough points to form a circle with all the points lying flat (24 points with ⅞" [2.2 cm] ribbon and 27 points with 1½" [4 cm] ribbon). Continue to take a stitch into each tip of the folds with the threaded needle. Pull thread firmly at each point to hold the petals snug against each other. It can be a little tricky to hold the cockade as you complete folding the points. Use clothespins to hold groups of points out of the way as you continue to fold and stitch the ribbon.

7. Join the start and end points with a stitch to make a circle of points. This circle will be at the center of the cockade, on the wrong side. Pass the thread around the circle, through all the tips of the points one more time and tighten the stitches. Knot to secure and trim excess thread.

8. Turn cockade over to the right side. Trim excess ribbon ¼" (6 mm) beyond the edge of the ribbon at the last folded point.

9. Insert raw edge coming out of the last fold into the fold of the first point. Use the tip of your scissors or a pin to tuck the raw edge evenly into the first fold. Secure the raw edge with a few stitches at each end to create a seamless circle of points.

10. If desired, slipstitch a circle of buckram to the back of the cockade and sew a button to the center of the right side.

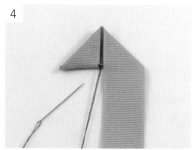

4

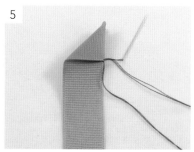

5

RIBBONS AND SUPPLIES

ribbon with enough body to hold a soft crease: ¾ yd (71 cm) ⅞" (2.2 cm) ribbon will make a 2¼" (5.5 cm) rosette.

2 needles and thread

2

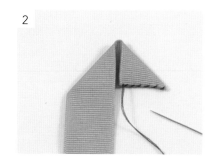

6

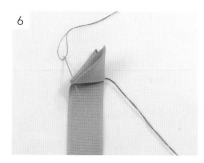

1

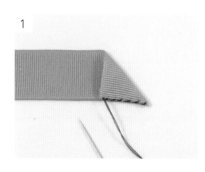

3

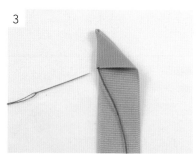

7

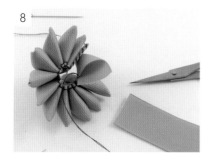

8

9

10

11

When selecting ribbon for this cockade, keep in mind that solid colors will show off the folding pattern, while stripes will create an interesting pattern that radiates out from the center of the cockade. Wire-edge ribbons may be used if the wires are removed from both edges.

Instructions

1. Turn under the raw edge ¼" (6 mm) at one end of the ribbon and press. With the wrong side up and the end to the right, fold down the turned back edge of the ribbon to align with the lower selvage edge. With thread doubled in needle, start at the point of the triangle just formed and slipstitch the pressed end to the selvage edge. End stitching at the inner side of the triangle. Secure thread but do not cut. Leave threaded needle hanging.

2. With the working end of the ribbon to the left, fold the ribbon down to form a large triangle. Leave a small space between the ribbon edges. This gap allows for the next fold of the ribbon.

3. Fold the large triangle in half to the right, with the gap at the inside center. Align the diagonal folds. Insert the threaded needle into the lower end of the fold and secure with a stitch. Do not cut thread. Leave needle hanging. One full point has been made.

4. Rotate the upper point of the triangle 90 degrees to the left. Make another triangle by folding the ribbon down and to the left, leaving a small gap between the ribbon edges.

5. Fold the large triangle in half and to the left, with the gap at the inside center. Align the diagonal folds. Insert the threaded needle into the end of the fold and secure the ribbon with a stitch. Leave the threaded needle hanging.

6. Take a second threaded needle and insert it into the center tip of the first point and then into the tip of the point you have just folded. This stitching will hold together the points at the center of the rosette. Leave the threaded needle hanging.

7. Repeat steps 2 to 6 until you have completed 12 points. Continue to take a stitch into each point at the lower edge of the triangle with the first threaded needle. Continue to insert the second needle into the center tip of each point to connect one right next to the other. Pull threads firmly to hold the points snug against each other. It can be a little tricky to hold the cockade as you complete the folding of the points. As long as you have secured each point at the base and at the tip, the points will align at the end.

8. When you have completed the last point, trim ribbon ¼" (6 mm) past the bottom of the last fold.

9. Turn raw edge to the inside of the last point and secure with a slipstitch.

10. Make a circle by joining the slipstitched edges of the first and last petal sections and secure with a few stitches. Knot and trim excess thread. This will be the bottom of the rosette.

11. Join the center tips of the rosette into a circle. Pull the thread tightly to push all the tips together. Secure thread and trim excess.

STAR-POINT COCKADE WITH LOOPS

RIBBONS AND SUPPLIES

ribbon with enough body to hold a soft crease: 2¼ yd (2.1 m) of 1½" (4 cm) ribbon and 1⅔ yd (1.5 m) of ⅝" (1.5 cm) ribbon will make a 4½" (11.5 cm) cockade.

2 needles and thread

3½" (9 cm) circle of buckram

3¾" (9.5 cm) circle of felt

button

When selecting ribbon for this cockade, keep in mind that solid colors will show off the folding pattern, while stripes will create an interesting pattern that radiates out from the center.

Instructions

1. Following the instructions on page 98, use the 1½" (10 cm) ribbon to make a Star-Point Cockade with 24 points.

2. Position the buckram circle on the back of the cockade and slipstitch each point to the circle.

3. Cut the ⅝" (1.5 cm) ribbon into twenty-four 2½" (6.5 cm) lengths. Fold each length in half and sew the ends together. Insert a loop into each space between points of the cockade. Stitch the raw edges onto the buckram, aligning the outer edge of the loops with the edge of the buckram.

4. Cover the buckram circle with the felt circle. Slip-stitch the edge of the felt to the loops and points, catching only the underside of the ribbons so no stitches will show on the right side.

5. Sew a button to the center. Pull stitches tight to the back and secure. This will create a swirl pattern of folds radiating out from the center.

1

2

3

4

When selecting ribbon for this cockade, keep in mind that solid colors will show off the folding pattern, while stripes will create an interesting pattern that radiates out from the center of the cockade. Wire-edge ribbons may be used if the wires are removed from both edges.

Instructions

1. Following steps 1 to 7 on page 98, make a Star-Point Cockade with 16 points. Follow steps 8 to 10 to finish the raw ribbon edge at the bottom of the cockade. Leave the second threaded needle in the top points of the cockade.

2. Fold the outside tip of the first point into the center of the cockade and stitch with the threaded needle to hold in place.

3. Bring the needle through the top of the second point. Fold the outside tip of the third point into the center of the cockade. Stitch to hold it in place.

RIBBONS AND SUPPLIES

ribbon with enough body to hold a soft crease: 1½ yd (1.4 m) of 1½" (4 cm) ribbon will make a 3½" (9 cm) cockade.

2 needles and thread

button

4. Continue to fold and stitch alternating points into the center of the cockade. The finished cockade will have eight outside points. Tighten the thread at the center of the cockade and secure thread. Sew a button to the center of the cockade.

Ribbon Sculptures

Ribbon sculptures are made by folding, looping, and gluing ribbons into shapes that represent objects, characters, and animals. They are fun to make and are perfect for hair accessories, pins, ornaments, scrapbook pages, greeting cards, gift bags, napkin rings, and more.

The best type of ribbon to use for making ribbon sculptures is usually polyester grosgrain. It has enough body and texture to hold the shape of the finished sculpture. But other ribbons can also be used, especially when you want a dressier or fancier effect, such a satin poinsettia or an embellishment for a fairy princess with a glitzy dress. Hot glue is the best glue to use as it sets up quickly and you do not have to wait for sections to dry before moving onto the next step.

Since ribbon sculptures often require that the cut edges of the ribbon be exposed, it is important that the raw edges be sealed to prevent fraying (page 140). This is especially true for any ribbon sculpture that will get a lot of wear or might be washed.

Ribbon sculptures are quick to make and because they require so little ribbon and not much else, they are an inexpensive yet very effective way to use narrow ribbons you may have left over from other projects. The samples shown here will get you started, but you can design many variations by just changing ribbon colors and sizes, inserting additional loops and folds, or gluing on a little embellishment.

1

TIP

Instead of the rolled ribbon center, glue or sew a button to the center of the petals.

2

RIBBONS AND SUPPLIES

grosgrain ribbon for petals, 18" (45.5 cm) of ⅜" (1 cm)

grosgrain ribbon for center, 12" (30.5 cm) of ⅜" (1 cm)

grosgrain ribbon for leaves and stem, 12" (30.5 cm) of ⅜" (1 cm), optional

hot glue gun and glue sticks

Instructions

1. Cut petal ribbon into three 6" (15 cm) lengths. Form each into a figure eight shape and glue at the center.

2. Overlap the centers of the figure eight shapes and glue, making sure that all the petals are evenly spaced around the flower.

3. Roll and glue the center ribbon into a tight spiral. Glue to the center of the flower.

4. To make a stem and leaves, cut ribbon in half. From one length, make a figure eight shape for the leaves. Glue the center of the leaves to the remaining length for the stem. Place the leaves 1½" (4 cm) from one end of the stem ribbon. Fold and glue the stem ribbon in half, over the center of the leaves.

5. Glue the top of the stem to the back of the flower.

3

4

BUTTERFLY

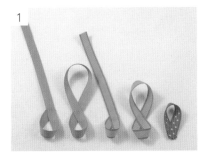

Instructions

1. Cut outer wing ribbon in half. Fold and glue two matching figure eight shapes with one loop smaller than the other. Cut the middle ribbon in half. Fold and glue two figure eight shapes to fit inside the outer wings. Cut the inner wing ribbon in half and fold and glue each length into a loop.

2. Overlap outer wings on a diagonal to form the butterfly shape. Glue at the center.

3. Position the middle wings inside the outer wings. Glue at the center.

4. Glue the inner wings inside the upper wings.

5. Fold the antennae ribbon in half and glue to the top center of the wings. Cut ends on a sharp diagonal. Make curled Korker Ribbon (page 123) for the body ribbon. When heat set and cooled, cut a 2" (5 cm) length and glue it to center of the butterfly. Seal exposed ribbon ends.

RIBBONS AND SUPPLIES

grosgrain ribbon for outer wings: 17" (43 cm) of ⅜" (1 cm)

grosgrain ribbon for middle wings: 14" (35.5 cm) of ⅜" (1 cm)

grosgrain ribbon for inner wings: 7" (18 cm) of ⅜" (1 cm)

grosgrain ribbon for body: 6" (15 cm) of ¼" (6 mm)

grosgrain ribbon for antennae: 2" (5 cm) of ⅛" (3 mm)

hot glue gun and glue sticks

¼" (6 mm) wood dowel

clear nail polish or Fray Check

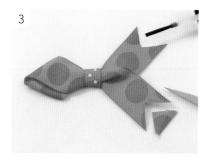

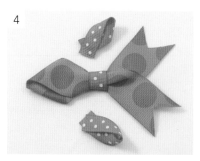

RIBBONS AND SUPPLIES

grosgrain ribbon, 8" (20.5 cm) of ⅞" (2.2 cm)

grosgrain ribbon, 6" (15 cm) of ⅜" (1 cm)

pin

hot glue gun and glue sticks

needle and thread

clear nail polish or Fray Check

7 mm wiggly eye

Instructions

1. Mark the center of the ⅞" (2.2 cm) ribbon length with a pin. Cross the ribbon ends to create the body of the fish. Allow for a small opening at the center fold to suggest the fish's mouth. Add a drop of glue where the ribbons overlap and also on the back of the fold to hold the ribbons in place.

2. Pinch the middle of the fish and sew a few stitches to gather up the ribbon and create the fish's tail fins.

3. Glue a length of ⅜" (1 cm) ribbon at the top of the fins, covering the stitches. Cut the ends of the tail fins into an inverted V and seal.

4. Cut the remaining ⅜" (1 cm) ribbon in half. Overlap and glue the ends on both lengths to form two loops for the top and bottom fins.

5. Glue the fins to the back of the fish. Glue the eye to the fish's head.

BEETLE BUG

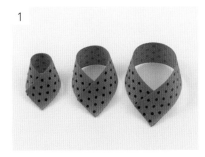

1

2

3

4

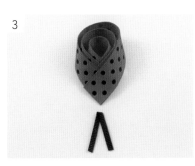

5

Instructions

1. For large bug, cut ⅝" (1.5 cm) ribbon into three lengths: 3" (7.5 cm), 4" (10 cm), and 5" (12.5 cm). For small bug, cut ⅜" (1 cm) ribbon into three lengths: 2" (5 cm), 3" (7.5 cm), and 4" (10 cm). Overlap the ends of each length to make three loops for each bug.

2. To make the bug body, glue the medium loop over the small loop and the large loop over the medium loop. Position the loops so that the overlapped ends are just a little bit above each other.

RIBBONS AND SUPPLIES

12" (30.5 cm) of ⅝" (1.5 cm) grosgrain ribbon for large bug; 9" (23cm) of ⅜" (1cm) grosgrain ribbon for small bug

2" (5 cm) of ⅝" (1.5 cm) black grosgrain ribbon for large bug; 1½" (4 cm) of ⅜" (1 cm) black grosgrain ribbon for small bug

2" (5 cm) of ⅛" (3 mm) black grosgrain ribbon for antennae

hot glue gun and glue sticks

3. Fold antennae ribbon into an inverted V. Glue at the center.

4. Glue the antennae to the back of the loop points. Center and glue the remaining black ribbon to the front of the loop points.

5. Bring excess black ribbon to the back of the bug and glue. Trim antennae ribbons to a point.

STRAWBERRIES

RIBBONS AND SUPPLIES

11" (28 cm) of 1½" (4 cm) grosgrain ribbon for large strawberry,
7" (18 cm) of ⅞" (2.2 cm) ribbon for medium strawberry

4" (10 cm) of ⅞" (2.2 cm) green grosgrain ribbon for large leaves,
3" (7.5 cm) of ⅝" (1.5 cm) ribbon for medium leaves

fusible web adhesive tape

iron

hot glue and glue sticks

clear nail polish or Fray Check

Instructions

1. Fold strawberry ribbon in half. Following manufacturer's instructions, iron fusible web adhesive tape to the inside of one half of the folded ribbon. Remove backing paper and fold ribbon in half. Fuse to create a double-sided ribbon length.

2. Fold the cut end of the fused ribbon up at an angle. Fold and align the folded end perpendicularly to the cut end to create an angled loop in the shape of a strawberry. Glue to hold.

3. For large leaves, cut ribbon into a 2½" (6.5 cm) length and a 1½" (4 cm) length for the stem. For medium leaves, cut ribbon into a 2" (5 cm) length and a 1" (2.5 cm) length for the stem. Cut both ends of the leaf ribbon into an inverted V. Cut one end of the stem ribbon into an inverted V. Seal all cut ends.

4. Fold leaf ribbon in half and glue to hold. Pinch the straight end of the stem ribbon together and glue.

5. With the leaves pointed down, glue them to the top of the strawberry. Glue the stem to the top of the leaves.

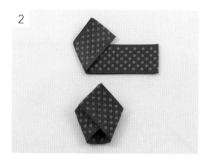

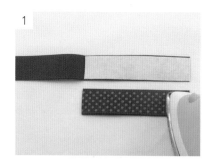

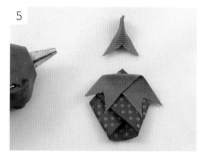

1

2

3

4

Instructions

1. Following instructions on page 85, make a set of double Folded Petal Leaves with the ⅝" (1.5 cm) ribbon. Sew the leaves at the center with a few stitches. Pull to gather. Knot thread and trim excess.

2. Fold ¼" (6 mm) ribbon around center of leaves and glue. Each end of the ribbon should angle out from the bottom of the leaves to form the stems for the cherries.

3. Cut red ribbon in half. From each length, make a cherry by rolling the ribbon around itself, gluing as needed to hold the rolled ribbon into a tight spiral.

4. Glue the ribbon cherries to the ends of the stems.

RIBBONS AND SUPPLIES

7" (18 cm) of ⅝" (1.5 cm) green grosgrain ribbon

4½" (11.5 cm) of ¼" (6 mm) green grosgrain ribbon

1½ yd (4 cm) of ⅜" (1 cm) red grosgrain ribbon

needle and thread

hot glue gun and glue sticks

RIBBONS AND SUPPLIES

10" (25.5 cm) of ⅝" (1.5 cm) grosgrain ribbon for the head

8" (20.5 cm) of ⅜" (1 cm) grosgrain ribbon for the ears

6" (15 cm) of ¼" (6 mm) ribbon for the bow

two 7 mm wiggly eyes

⅛" (3 mm) pom-pom

hot glue gun and glue sticks

TIP

Create different animals, such as a cat or a bunny, by using the same basic head shape and changing the shape and placement of the ears.

Instructions

1. Cut ⅝" (1.5 cm) ribbon into one 3½" (9 cm) length and two 3¼" (8.5 cm) lengths. Roll each length into a circle. Overlap ends ¼" (6 mm) and glue.

2. To create the dog's head, position the smaller circles inside each side of the larger circle. Angle them down slightly and glue.

3. To make the ears, fold the ⅜" (1 cm) ribbon into a figure eight loop and glue at the center.

4. Glue the ears to the top of the dog's head. Glue the eyes to the middle of the center head ribbon loop. Glue the pom-pom below the eyes for the nose. Tie the ¼" (6 mm) ribbon into a bow and glue it at the bottom of the head.

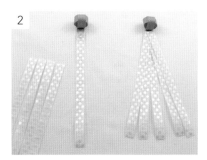

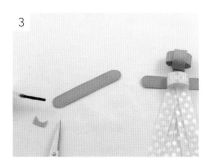

Instructions

1. From body ribbon, cut two lengths for the head: 2½" (6.5 cm) and 3" (7.5 cm). Roll and glue the shorter length into a circle. Roll and glue a circle about the same size with the longer length, leaving ½" (1.3 cm) hanging down for the neck. Glue the circle inside the circle with the neck.

2. Cut five 6" (15 cm) lengths of dress ribbon. Glue one length straight down from the neck ribbon. Glue two lengths out to each side, angling them slightly away from the center dress ribbon.

3. Cut a 2" (5 cm) length of dress ribbon. Glue one end to the back of the neck. Bring it around to the front and glue the other end to the back, forming a circle for the top of the dress. For the arms, round the ends of the remaining body ribbon and seal the cut edges. Glue the arms to the back of the neck.

4. Cut the remaining dress ribbon in half. Form each length into a circle and glue. Slide the circles over the arms and glue for sleeves. Fold back loops of the hanging dress ribbon to the back and glue.

5. Make curled Korker Ribbon (page 123) for the hair. When heat set and cooled, cut and glue a few curls to the top of the head. Glue the remaining curled ribbon to the top and sides of the head. Seal exposed ribbon ends.

6. Form sheer ribbon into a four-loop bow. Gather in the center with a few stitches. Glue to the back of the fairy for wings.

RIBBONS AND SUPPLIES

8" (20.5 cm) of ⅜" (1 cm) grosgrain ribbon for body

1 yd (.9 m) of ⅜" (1 cm) ribbon for dress

18" (45.5 cm) of ⅝" (1.5 cm) sheer ribbon for wings

15" (38 cm) of ⅜" (1 cm) grosgrain ribbon for hair

needle and thread

clear nail polish or Fray Check

¼" (6 mm) wood dowel

TIP

Create different characters, such as a bird or a snowman, by using the same basic shape and adding ribbons for feathers, ears, top hat, etc.

Instructions

1. Cut ⅜" (1 cm) ribbon into three lengths: 2" (5 cm), 3" (7.5 cm), and 4" (10 cm). Overlap and glue the ends of each length to make three loops. To make the bunny body, glue the medium loop over the small loop and the large loop over the medium loop. Position the loops so that the overlapped ends are just a little bit above each other.

2. Cut a 7½" (19 cm) length of ⅜" (1 cm) ribbon. Glue one end to the top of the overlapped body loops. Form a slightly larger loop around the body and glue at the top. Fold the remainder of the ribbon forward, around, and to the back, to make a figure eight shape and create the bunny head.

3. Cut remaining ⅜" (1 cm) ribbon in half. Cut ¼" (6 mm) inner ear ribbon in half. Overlap the ends of each length and glue to create outer and inner ears. Glue the inner ear loops inside the outer ear loops.

4. Glue the ears to the top of the bunny, flattening the head ribbon loop. Glue the eyes and pom-pom nose to the bunny head. Tie the ¼" (6 mm) ribbon into a bow and glue it under the bunny head.

RIBBONS AND SUPPLIES

22½" (57 cm) of ⅜" (1 cm) grosgrain ribbon

5" (12.5 cm) of ¼" (6 mm) ribbon for inner ears

6" (15 cm) of ¼" (6 mm) ribbon for bow

two 7 mm wiggly eyes

⅛" (3 mm) pom-pom

hot glue gun and glue sticks

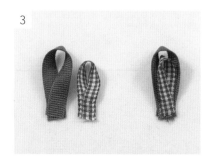

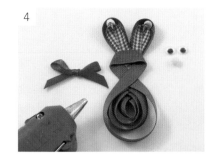

Instructions

1. Cut white ribbon into two lengths: 6" (15 cm) and 7" (18 cm). Seal the ends of both lengths, along with the ends of the red ribbon. Center the 7" (18 cm) white ribbon onto the red ribbon. Add a small drop of glue to hold at the middle. Center the 6" (15 cm) white ribbon on top of the 7" (18 cm) white ribbon. Add a small drop of glue to hold. Keeping the ribbons in order, bring the cut ends of all three ribbon lengths together at each end. Apply glue between all three ribbon lengths from the ends toward the centers ½" (1.3 cm).

2. To make the apple shape, roll the glued ends of the ribbon lengths toward the center. Glue the red ribbon sides together from about ½" (1.3 cm) in and out toward the ends.

3. Cut a 1" (2.5 cm) length of brown ribbon and seal the ends. Pinch the selvage edges together and glue to form the stem. Seal the ends of the green

ribbon. Overlap the ends and glue to form the leaf. Glue the stem and leaf to the top of the apple.

4. Cut the remaining brown ribbon in half. Roll and glue each length into a seed shape. Glue one seed to each side of the apple center.

RIBBONS AND SUPPLIES

8" (20.5 cm) of ⅜" (1 cm) red grosgrain ribbon

13" (33 cm) of ⅜" (1 cm) white grosgrain ribbon

6" (15 cm) of ⅜' (1 cm) brown grosgrain ribbon

2¼" (5.5 cm) of ⅜" (1 cm) green grosgrain ribbon

hot glue gun and glue sticks

clear nail polish or Fray Check

WOVEN HEART

RIBBONS AND SUPPLIES

7" (18 cm) each of two colors of ⅜" grosgrain ribbon; or 14" (35.5 cm) of one color

clear nail polish or Fray Check

hot glue and glue sticks

Instructions

1. Cut each ribbon into one 4" (10 cm) length and one 3" (7.5 cm) length. If using one color of ribbon, cut two 4" (10 cm) lengths and two 3" (7.5 cm) lengths. Seal all cut ends. Overlap the long ribbons at one end to form a point. Place the right ribbon on top of the left. Glue.

2. Matching ribbon colors (if you are using two colors), place the short ribbons on top of the long ribbons, aligning the cut ends at the point. Glue the left ribbon to the point and then the right. Glue only at the point, leaving the rest of the ribbon lengths free for weaving.

3. Fold the top left ribbon down to form a loop. Glue it on the right top ribbon, aligning the cut end with the selvage edge.

4. Fold the top right ribbon down. Pass it through the loop and align the end under the top left ribbon. Glue.

5. Fold the right bottom ribbon down to create a loop. Weave it through the left loop and align the end over the top left ribbon. Glue.

6. Fold the left bottom ribbon down to create a loop. Weave it under the large loop and over the small loop. Align the end under the top right ribbon. Glue.

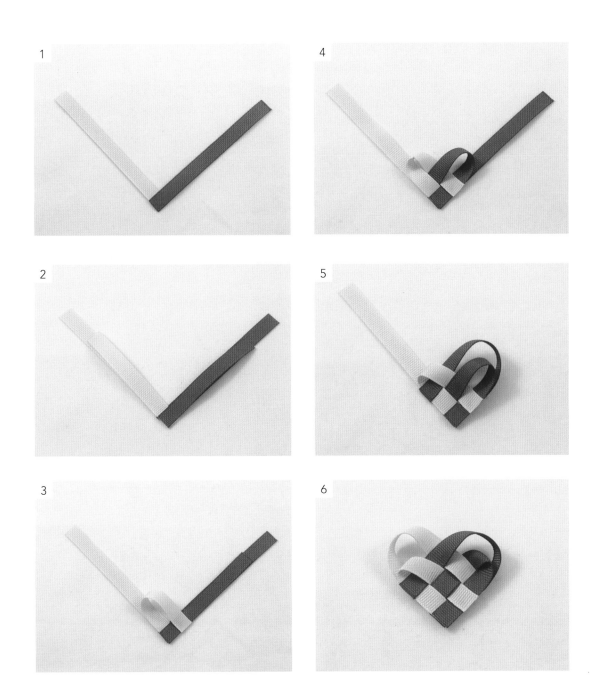

RIBBONS AND SUPPLIES

26" (66 cm) of ⅜" (1 cm) grosgrain ribbon

clear nail polish or Fray Check

hot glue and glue sticks

Instructions

1. Cut five 5" (12.5 cm) lengths of ribbon. Seal all cut ends.

2. Lay two ribbons vertically on work surface, selvage edges right next to each other. Weave a third ribbon length horizontally over the left vertical ribbon and under the right. Weave another length under the left vertical ribbon and over the right. Center the woven square, and snug the ribbons close together.

3. Fold the left vertical ribbon down to the left to form a loop. Align the cut endwith the inside selvage edge of the top horizontal ribbon. Glue it to the top horizontal ribbon. Rotate the woven ribbons 90 degrees to the right.

4. Follow step 3 three more times, creating a total of four loops.

5. Fold the right vertical ribbon donw and to the right. Pass it through the loop and to the back of the top horizontal ribbon. Align the cut end with the selvage edge and glue. Rotate the woven ribbons 90 degrees to the left.

6. Follow step 5 three more times, creating four clover petals. To make the stem, fold the remaining ribbon lenght in half and glue. Glue the stem to the back of the petals.

3

4

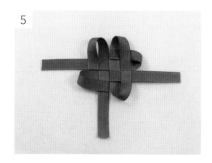

5

2

6

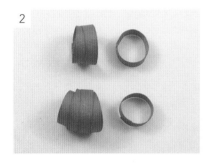

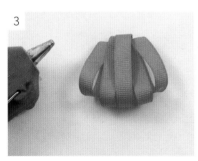

Instructions

1. Cut orange ribbon into one 4" (10 cm) length, two 3¾" (9.5 cm) lengths, and two 3½" (9 cm) lengths. Form a ring with each length, overlapping the ends ¼" (6 mm). Glue to hold.

2. Position a middle size ring on each side of the large ring. Glue them halfway inside the large ring and angled out to the side. In the same way, position and glue the small rings inside each middle ring, creating the pumpkin shape.

3. Slightly flatten the pumpkin shape at the top and add a drop of glue at the center to hold the shape.

4. Cut green ribbon in half. Cut a deep inverted V into both ends of one length and seal. Angle and fold ribbon in half and glue to the top of the pumpkin. Pinch one end of the remaining length in half and glue. Cut a deep inverted V into the other end. Seal both ends. Glue to the top of the pumpkin.

RIBBONS AND SUPPLIES

18½" (47 cm) of ⅜" (1 cm) orange grosgrain ribbon for pumpkin

4½" (11.5 cm) of ⅜" (1 cm) green grosgrain ribbon for stem

hot glue gun and glue sticks

clear nail polish or Fray Check

TIP

Make the pumpkin into a jack-o'-lantern by gluing or sewing small black beads onto the ribbon for the face. Or, draw the face onto the ribbon with a permanent marker or paint.

2

3

4

RIBBONS AND SUPPLIES

19½" (49.5 cm) of ⅝" (1.5 cm) red
satin ribbon

4" (10 cm) of ⅝" (1.5 cm) green satin
ribbon

clear nail polish or Fray Check

needle and thread

small gold beads

Instructions

1. To make the poinsettia petals, cut the red ribbon
into four 3" (7.5 cm) lengths and three 2½" (6.5 cm)
lengths. Cut the ends of each length into a point
and seal.

2. Sew the four longer petals together at the center
with long stitches. Pull thread to gather. Fan the
petals out evenly around the center and secure with
a few stitches. Do the same with the three shorter
petals.

3. Sew the shorter petals to the center of the longer
petals. Adjust and stitch the petals so they fan out
evenly around the center.

4. To make the leaves, cut the ends of the green
ribbon length into a point and seal. Gather at the
center with a few stitches and sew to the back of
the petals.

5. Sew beads to the center of the poinsettia.

1

5

CHRISTMAS TREE

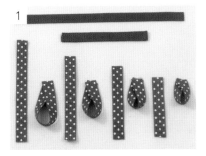

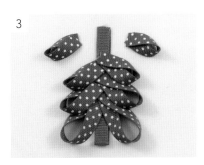

Instructions

1. Fold and glue tree trunk ribbon in half. Cut lengths of ribbon for tree branches: two 3½" (9 cm), two 3" (7.5 cm), two 2½" (6.5 cm), and two 2" (5 cm). Overlap the ends of each branch ribbon length and glue to form loops.

2. Glue one of the largest loops to the trunk 1½" (4 cm) above the fold. Angle the loop down and to the left. Position and glue the other largest loop down and to the right, overlapping the raw ends of the previous loop.

3. Continue to glue the remaining 3 sets of loops to the tree trunk, alternating one on each side and decreasing in size as the branches are glued up the trunk.

4. Trim the top of the trunk into a point. Glue the star gem or button to the top of the tree.

RIBBONS AND SUPPLIES

22" (56 cm) of ⅜" (1 cm) ribbon for tree branches

6" (15 cm) of ⅜" (1 cm) ribbon for tree trunk

hot glue gun and glue sticks

star gem or button

TIP

A small bow can be glued to the top of the tree instead of the star. Small beads can be sewn or glued to the tree as ornaments.

Beads and Baubles

In addition to ribbon trims, braids, rosettes, leaves, and ribbon sculptures, there are a few more ribbon embellishments that are fun to add to your library of techniques. I call them Beads and Baubles, and you'll find instructions for them in this section.

These embellishments are perfect to use for jewelry projects and fashion accessories. You can combine rolled ribbon beads with ribbon charms and ribbon beading. A single Galette, which looks like a flattened pleated ribbon pancake, makes a beautiful pendant. A group of ribbon Chinese Cross Knots would be lovely across the front of a clutch bag or along the edge of a cardigan sweater. And don't forget to add some bows to your toes—embellish your shoes with ribbon Pom-Poms.

Ribbon Beads and Baubles can also decorate your home. Layered and embellished ribbon tassels are elegant accents and Paddlewheels and Knotted Ribbon Stars make unique Christmas ornaments.

Many of these embellishments do not require much yardage, and they are great ways to use up the little pieces of ribbon that are just too precious to toss. Who needs diamonds and pearls when you can make special Beads and Baubles from ribbon?

POM-POM

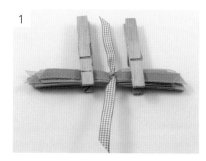

RIBBONS AND SUPPLIES

Twenty 5" (12.5 cm) lengths of various ribbons will make a 4" (10 cm) pom-pom. Choose coordinating patterns and styles, ranging in width from ¼" to ½" (6 mm to 1.3 cm).

7" (18 cm) of coordinating ¼" to ½" (6 mm to 1.3 cm) ribbon

2 clothes pins

Instructions

1. Stack the ribbon lengths on top of each other in an attractive order, varying colors and types of ribbons. Use clothespins to hold the stack together on each side of the center. Tightly tie the 7" (18 cm) ribbon length around the center of the stack.

2. Unclip the ribbons from the left side of the stack and fold all but the bottom two ribbons over to the right. Reposition the right clip to hold all the ribbons. Tie the bottom two ribbons together with an overhand knot, pulling the ends tight until the knot slides into the center of the stack.

3. Unclip two ribbons at a time and tie them tightly together with an overhand knot at the center of the stack. Continue until four ribbons remain from the left side.

4. In the same way, tie the ribbons on the right side, two at a time, until four ribbons from the right remain.

5. Unclip the remaining eight ribbon lengths. Starting with the two center lengths, knot the remaining ribbons together in pairs, one from each side. Make sure each knot slides into the center to fill the center of the pom-pom. Spread out all the ribbon tails around the center. Trim the ribbon lengths to create a round pom-pom shape.

KORKER POM-POM

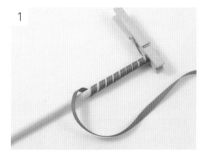

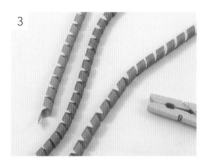

TIP

Make sure the ribbon you select is 100% polyester. Other types of ribbon may not set into curls when heated in the oven.

Instructions

1. Wrap each ribbon tightly around a dowel. Use clothespins to secure the ends of the ribbon.

2. Line the center oven rack with foil and preheat the oven to 275°F (135°C). Place the dowels into the oven and bake 15 to 20 minutes, checking often to make sure the ribbons do not start to discolor.

3. Remove the dowels from the oven and allow them to cool completely. Remove the clothespins and gently unravel the curled Korker Ribbon off the dowels.

4. Cut Korker Ribbon into fifteen 3" (7.5 cm) lengths. Insert the threaded needle into the center of each length. Gather the curled ribbons into a fluffy pom-pom and secure with a few stitches.

RIBBONS AND SUPPLIES

5 yd (4.6 m) of ¼" to ⅜" (6 mm to 1 cm) 100% polyester grosgrain ribbons will make a 3" (7.5 cm) pom-pom. The sample shown was made with one yard (0.92 m) each of five different colors.

¼" (6 mm) clean, unpainted wooden dowels

clothespins

aluminum foil

oven

needle and thread

CHINESE CROSS KNOT

Use a two-sided ribbon, such as velvet, for this knot. The two different textures make it easier to see that the ribbon is properly positioned as it is knotted.

Instructions

1. With the right side down, pin the center of the ribbon to the pinable surface. The ribbon tails should point up.

2. Work with the left tail to create a Z shape around the right tail. With the right side of the ribbon down, bring the left ribbon under the right tail to make the bottom of the Z. With the right side of the ribbon up, bring it diagonally over the right tail to make the center of the Z. With the right side of the ribbon down, bring it under the right tail to make the top of the Z. Pin the ribbon at the corners of the Z.

3. Fold down the right tail diagonally over all three sections of the Z. The right side of the ribbon should face up.

4. Fold the right ribbon (which has now moved to the left side), under the bottom of the Z, right side down. Bring the right ribbon under the diagonal of the Z and over the top of the Z, continuing to keep the right side of the ribbon down.

5. Remove pins and carefully pull on both tails to form a loose knot.

6. Turn knot over to the right side. Continue to pull tails and adjust ribbon, making sure it lies flat throughout the cross.

7. Secure the ribbon at the center of the knot with a few stitches. If desired, sew a button or bead to the center. Trim excess ribbon then fold and stitch to the back of the knot.

RIBBONS AND SUPPLIES

1 yd (0.92 m) of ⅞" (2.2 cm) ribbon will make a 1¾" (4.5 cm) knot. 24" (61 cm) of ½" (1.3 cm) ribbon will make a 1" (2.5 cm) knot.

pins

pinable surface such as an ironing board or piece of foam core

needle and thread

small bead or button (optional)

1

2

3

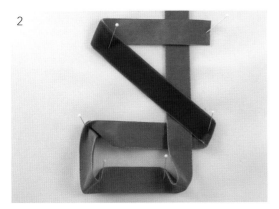

4

5

6

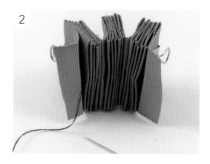

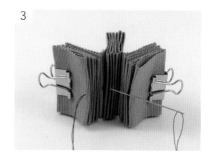

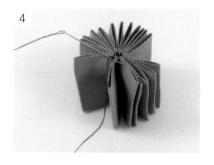

RIBBONS AND SUPPLIES

24" (61 cm) of ⅞" (2.2 cm) ribbon
or 1 yd (0.92 m) of 1½" (4 cm)
ribbon that makes crisp pleats,
such as grosgrain or petersham

needle and thread

ruler

pins

binder clips or clothes pins

Instructions

1. Refer to the instructions on page 36 for making
Paddlewheel Trim. Follow step **1.** Continue to fold
a total of 12 pleats if using ⅞" (2.2 cm) ribbon and
18 pleats if using 1½" (4 cm) ribbon. Clip the pleats
together in two or three groups to hold.

2. Beginning at the second pleat, sew the folds
together at the center of the ribbon. Insert the
threaded needle just into each fold. Do not include
the last pleat. Do not cut thread. Trim the ribbon
ends to half the depth of the pleats.

3. Fold back the trimmed ends inside the first and
last pleats. Sew the center of the last pleat to the
center of the first pleat. Do not cut thread.

4. Remove clips. Tighten thread to bring pleats
together. Knot and trim excess thread, creating a
circle of pleats. Sew the pleats together at the top
and the bottom at the inside of the circle.

5. Open each pleat and tuck both ends toward the
center. Use the tip of a small pair of scissors to fold
the ribbon into position. Stitch through all folds
near the top and bottom edges to hold the ribbon
secure and create the paddlewheel.

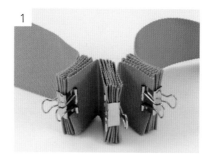

1

2

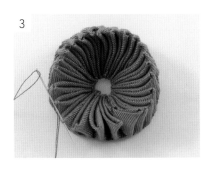

3

4

TIP

The cockade does not have to be flattened. The spiral top created in step 4 can be used as an embellishment on its own.

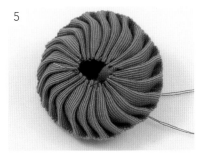

5

RIBBONS AND SUPPLIES

ribbon with enough body to hold a soft crease, such as petersham or grosgrain: 1½ yd (1.4 m) of ⅞" (2.2 cm) ribbon will make a 2" (5 cm) galette

needle and thread

clothespins

Instructions

1. Follow steps 1 to 9 on page 96 for making a Folded Cockade. Turn the cockade upside down with the flat side face-up. With thread doubled in needle, sewing running stitches through the center point of all folds.

2. Pull up the thread until the cockade forms a cup and the new bottom lies flat. Knot thread and trim excess.

3. Connect the tips of all the standing points with a running stitch.

4. Pull thread tight to make the center the same size as the center on the bottom of the cockade. Knot thread and trim excess. A spiral top shape has been formed.

5. Bring the top and bottom centers together and flatten the spiral top to form a doughnut. Form the cockade into a pancake shape, twisting and pushing the center folds until they lie smooth. Sew the centers together with a few stitches to hold the pancake flat.

WRAPPED TASSEL

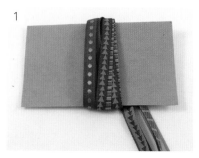

RIBBONS AND SUPPLIES

⅛" to ⅜" (3 mm to 1 cm) ribbons in a variety of types and coordinated colors. The exact yardage needed will depend upon the desired length and fullness of the finished tassel.

cardboard cut to the desired length of the tassel

needle and thread

Instructions

1. Hold the ribbons as a group and wrap them around the cardboard several times. The amount of ribbon wrapped onto the cardboard will determine the fullness of the tassel.

2. Cut a length of narrow ribbon for the tassel hanger. Against one edge of the cardboard, pass the hanger ribbon through all the loops. Tie the ribbon tightly to hold the loops.

3. Carefully remove the tassel from the cardboard. Wrap a length of ribbon around the tassel, just below the top. Tie the ribbon securely and add a few stitches to keep the ribbon wrap in place.

4. Trim the ribbon ends so that they do not hang below the ribbon loops.

5. If desired, cut the loops of the tassel. Trim the ribbon ends on a diagonal so they will not fray.

LAYERED TASSEL

Instructions

1. To make the tassel topper, glue the wheel to the bottom of the flower pot, taking care to align the holes. Paint the topper and allow to dry.

2. Cut an 18" (45.5 cm) length of ribbon for the tassel hanger. Use the large-eye needle to thread both ends of the ribbon through the hole in the topper. Tie ends together with an overhand knot. Pull up the ribbon loop so the knot rests against the inside of the topper.

3. Cut eight 6" (15 cm) lengths of ⅜" (1 cm) ribbon for the outer loops. Fold each length in half and glue the ends together. Evenly position the loops around the inside of the topper and glue the ends in place.

4. Cut eight 8" (20.5 cm) lengths of ⅝" (1.5 cm) ribbon for the inner loops. Fold each length in half and glue the ends together. Evenly position the loops around the inside of the topper and glue the ends in place over the previous loops.

5. Follow the instructions on page 63 for making Mix and Match Ribbon Fringe. Cut the ribbon into lengths 13½" (34.5 cm) long. Fold the lengths in half and sew them to the twill tape. Make 9" (23 cm) of fringe. Roll the fringe and glue the twill tape to create the inside tassel. Glue the tassel inside the topper, making sure that the outer and inner loops are out of the way.

RIBBONS AND SUPPLIES

⅛" to ⅝" (3 mm to 1.5 cm) ribbons of various types, in coordinated colors. The amount of ribbon needed will depend upon the desired size of the finished tassel and the types of ribbon selected.

2" (5 cm) unfinished wood flower pot

2" (5 cm) unfinished wood toy wheel

acrylic paint and paint brush

large-eye needle

½" (1.3 cm) twill tape

sewing machine and thread

hot glue gun and glue sticks

KNOTTED RIBBON STAR

RIBBONS AND SUPPLIES

24" (61 cm) of ⅝" (1.5 cm) ribbon will make a 3" (7.5 cm) star. 18" (45.5 cm) of ⅜" (1 cm) ribbon will make a 2" (5 cm) star.

fabric glue or hot glue gun and glue stick

Instructions

1. Hold one end of the ribbon between your index finger and thumb. The long end of the ribbon should point up from the tip of your index finger at a 45-degree angle. Wrap the ribbon around your index finger to create a loop. Remove your finger and tuck the working end of the ribbon through the loop, forming an overhand knot shaped like an X.

2. Pull the ribbon gently to flatten the knot near the end of the ribbon.

3. Continue to make five more overhand knots. Take care to tie all the knots in the same direction. Keep the knots flat and adjust each knot so that the bottom left side just touches the bottom right side of the previous knot. Use a pin to hold each knot in place as it is formed.

4. When all six knots are tied, trim the ribbons, leaving ¼" to ½" (6 mm to 1.3 cm) at each end. Remove pins from first and last knots and tuck the ribbon ends into the knots on the opposite sides, creating a ring and forming the six-knot star shape. Secure ribbon ends with a dot of glue.

ROLLED RIBBON BEADS

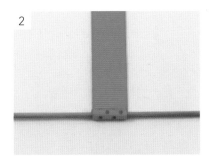

2

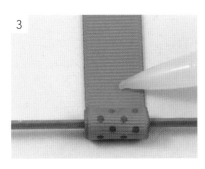

3

4

TIP

Roll narrower ribbons on top of wider ribbons to create a shaped bead.

Instructions

1. Decide how large you want the finished bead to be and cut a length of ribbon. Narrower ribbons can be cut into 2" to 3" (5 cm to 7.5 cm) lengths and wider ribbons into 4" to 6" (10 cm to 15 cm) lengths. Seal both ends of the ribbon.

2. Place the ribbon right-side down onto work surface. Fold one end of the ribbon over the skewer. Roll one full turn and apply a line of glue to the ribbon from edge to edge. Continue to roll the ribbon over the skewer to secure the first row of wrapping.

3. Carefully continue to roll the skewer and glue the ribbon around itself, making sure that both ribbon selvage edges are evenly aligned.

4. Apply a line of glue at the end of the ribbon and roll the bead back and forth several times to secure the seam. Allow the bead to dry completely on the skewer before removing it.

5. Small beads can be sewn to the finished beads to accent the design of the ribbon or to hide the ending seam. Beads can be sewn to the ends of the beads. A row or two of beads can be wrapped around the center of a rolled ribbon bead.

RIBBONS AND SUPPLIES

2" to 6" (5 cm to 15 cm) of any ribbon type or width. The exact amount needed will depend upon the desired thickness of the finished bead.

clear nail polish or Fray Check

bamboo skewer

fabric glue

small beads, beading needle and thread (optional)

RIBBON PENDANT

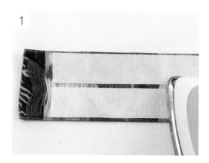

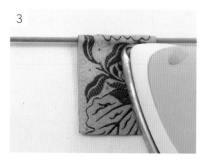

RIBBONS AND SUPPLIES

3½" (9 cm) of ⅞" (2.2 cm) ribbon or
4½" (11.5 cm) of 1½" (4 cm) ribbon

2¼" (5.5 cm) of ⅞" (2.2 cm) or 6½"
(16.5 cm) of ⅝" (1.5 cm) iron-on
adhesive tape

iron

sewing machine and thread

bamboo skewer

small beads, beading thread, and
needle (optional)

*For this pendant, select a stripe or jacquard ribbon
with an interesting woven design.*

Instructions

1. Following manufacturer's instructions, apply
iron-on adhesive to the back of the ribbon. If using
⅞" (2.2 cm) ribbon, center the ⅞" (2.2 cm) adhesive
onto the ribbon. If using 1½" (4 cm) ribbon, cut the
⅝" (1.5 cm) adhesive in half and center a piece near
each edge. Stop the adhesive ⅝" (1.5 cm) from each
end of the ribbon.

2. Remove backing from adhesive. Fold ribbon in
half, with right sides together, aligning cut ends.
Stitch ¼" from the end.

3. Trim seam allowance to ⅛" (3 mm). Turn ribbon
right side out. Position the seam to the top of the
pendant. Insert the skewer into the turned ribbon
circle and place it at the top, over the seam allowance. Roll the seam very slightly to the back. Align
the ribbon edges. With the skewer held in place,
fuse the layers together to create the pendant.
Place the edge of the iron right up to the edge of
the skewer.

4. Remove skewer, leaving an opening for stringing
the pendant onto a narrow cord, chain, or string of
beads. If desired, sew beads around the edges of
the pendant or into the design of the ribbon.

RIBBON CHARMS AND CONNECTORS

Instructions

1. Select a motif from the ribbon or determine the desired finished size of the charm or connector. Cut two ribbon lengths, allowing ¼" (6 mm) extra on each side for seams. Make sure both lengths are the same size.

2. Cut two pieces of interfacing ⅛" (3 mm) narrower than the ribbon width and ½" (1.3 cm) shorter than the cut lengths. Following manufacturer's instructions, center and fuse the interfacing onto the back of each ribbon length. Press the ¼" (6 mm) seam allowance on each cut end of the ribbon to the wrong side.

3. Place the wrong sides of the ribbon pieces together. Sew tiny slipstitches around all four sides, inserting one or two jump rings halfway into the seam and securely stitching them in place. If you are making a charm, sew one jump ring at the top

RIBBONS AND SUPPLIES

⅞" to 1½" (2.2 cm to 4 cm) ribbon. The exact length needed will depend upon the design of the ribbon and the desired size of the charm or connector.

heavy-weight iron-on interfacing

needle and thread

one or two 6 to 8 mm jump rings

small beads, beading thread, and needle (optional)

of the ribbon sandwich. If you are making a connector, sew one jump ring to each side of the ribbon sandwich.

4. If desired, add beads to the sides of the ribbon sandwich as you stitch it together. Beads can also be added to accent parts of the motifs within the ribbon.

ZIGZAG RIBBON BEADING

RIBBONS AND SUPPLIES

¼" to ⅝" (6 mm to 1.5 cm) ribbon, about two times the length of the desired finished beading

6 mm to 15 mm round beads or pearls

hand-sewing needle, small enough to pass through the holes in the beads

beading thread to match the ribbon

For best effect, select a double-sided ribbon, such as grosgrain, taffeta, or double-faced satin. The beads should be about the same size as the width of the ribbon.

Instructions

1. Decide where you want to begin adding beads onto the ribbon. With thread doubled and knotted in the needle, insert the needle into the ribbon at the chosen point. Take a small stitch back into the ribbon and string on the first bead. The bead will come down to cover the knot.

2. Bring the working end of the ribbon over the bead. Insert the needle at the point where the bead hole meets the center of the ribbon. Take one or two small stitches to hold the ribbon against the bead.

3. Thread the next bead onto the needle and place it against the ribbon. Bring the ribbon up and over the bead. Insert the needle where the hole meets the center of the ribbon. Take one or two small stitches to hold the ribbon against the bead.

4. Continue adding beads in this way. The ribbon will zigzag between the beads. As the beads are added, check to make sure that enough ribbon has been placed around each bead to hold the beads in a straight line.

5. End the beading by securely knotting the thread into the ribbon and then passing it through several beads before trimming away the excess.

> **TIP**
> If desired, begin and end the beading with an overhand knot in the ribbon. Hide the thread knots in the ribbon knots.

SCALLOP RIBBON BEADING

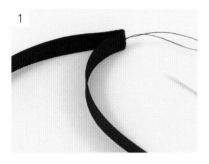

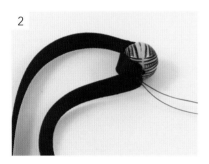

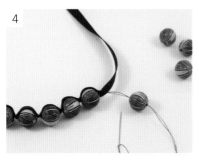

For this project, select a double-sided ribbon, such as grosgrain, taffeta, or double-faced satin. The total number of beads needed will depend upon the desired finish length of the beading. The beads should be a little larger than the width of the ribbon.

Instructions

1. Decide where you'd like to begin adding beads onto the ribbon. With thread doubled and knotted in the needle, insert the needle into the ribbon at the chosen point. Fold the ribbon back onto itself and take a few small stitches at the fold to hide the knot.

2. Thread the first bead onto the needle and bring it down to the ribbon. Bring the working end of the ribbon up and over the bead. Insert the needle into the ribbon and take one or two small stitches. Fold the ribbon back onto itself at this point. Take another one or two small stitches to secure the fold against the bead.

3. Add the second bead in the same way, keeping the ribbon folded back in the same direction so the ribbon remains on only one side of the beads.

4. Continue adding beads for the desired length of the beading. From time to time, check to make sure that enough ribbon has been placed against each bead and the beads are straight. When you hold up the beading by the ribbon ends, the weight of the beads should cause the beads to fall below the ribbon scallops.

5. End the beading by securely knotting the thread into the ribbon and then passing it through several beads before trimming away the excess.

RIBBONS AND SUPPLIES

¼" to ⅜" (6 mm to 1 cm) ribbon about 1½ times the length of the desired finished beading

10 mm to 16 mm round beads or pearls

hand-sewing needle, small enough to pass through the holes in the beads.

beading thread to match the color of the ribbon

FREEFORM RIBBON BEADING

RIBBONS AND SUPPLIES

¼" to ⅝" (6 mm to 1.5 cm) ribbon.

6 mm to 16 mm round beads or pearls

hand-sewing needle, small enough to pass through the holes in the beads

beading thread that matches the color of the ribbon

Instructions

Select a double-sided ribbon, such as grosgrain, taffeta, or double-faced satin for this project. The amount needed will depend upon how much ribbon is looped between the beads. The total number of beads needed will depend upon the desired finish length of the beading.

Instructions for One-Ribbon Freeform Beading

1. Knot the ribbon where you'd like to begin the beading. With thread doubled and knotted in the needle, insert the needle into the ribbon at the chosen point. Take a small stitch to secure the thread. Loop and twist the ribbon several times, passing the needle through each turn to hold. Thread on the first bead. Bring the working end of the ribbon over the bead, twisting it if desired. Insert the needle into the ribbon and take one or two small stitches to hold the ribbon in place.

2. Loop and twist the ribbon a few times in a free-form design before stringing on the second bead. The loops can be big or small, and formed in any direction.

3. Continue to make freeform loops, adding beads and working your way down the length of the ribbon until the beading is the desired length. At the end, tie an overhand knot in the ribbon close to the last loop. Secure the thread in the knot, trimming away the excess.

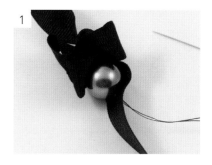

1

2

Instructions for Two-Ribbon Freeform Beading

1. Cut two lengths of ribbon. With thread doubled and knotted in the needle, insert the needle into the ribbon where you would like the beading to begin. Thread the first bead onto the needle and bring it down to the ribbon. Bring the working end of the ribbon that lies next to the bead over the bead. Insert the needle at the point where the bead hole meets the center of the ribbon. Take a few stitches to hold the ribbon in place against the bead.

2. Thread the second bead. Bring the working end of the other ribbon around the bead and insert the needle into the center of the ribbon, taking a few small stitches to hold the ribbon against the bead.

3. Thread the next bead. Bring the working end of the first ribbon around the bead. Insert needle into the center of the ribbon and take a few small stitches to hold. Continue to add beads. Alternate the ribbons as you bring them down and around each bead. The ribbons can be looped and twisted or held flat, as shown. When you reach the end, stitch the ribbons together, knot thread, and bury excess thread inside the beads and ribbon.

1

2

3

Technical Support

Ribbons

Of course the most important supply is the ribbon itself. There are many types available, in a wide variety of colors and textures and patterns. Ribbons fall into two categories. Woven edge ribbons are woven on a loom and have finished edges, or selvages. Cut-edge or craft ribbons, sometimes referred to as floral ribbons, are cut from fabric and are usually too stiff to be manipulated. For all the ribbon embellishments in this book, I have used woven ribbons.

Perhaps the most important thing to remember is to look for ribbons that can be easily folded, pleated, and gathered. Choose the best quality you can afford, as less expensive ribbons do not have a good feel and will not work as well for making the embellishments. Quality acetate, rayon, and silk ribbon, whether new or vintage, are good choices. Polyester ribbons will also work, although they may be a little thick or stiff for some embellishments. Avoid ribbons with printed designs, except perhaps for a mini dot ribbon. Printed ribbons are printed on only one side and oftentimes the wrong side of the ribbon will show on a created embellishment. Printed ribbons can be a bit stiff to fold and gather and care must be taken when ironing the printed ribbon to ensure that the design does not smear from the heat of the iron.

Many ribbons today have wire or monofilament edges, which help them to keep their shape when made into a bow. These ribbons can be used for making some ribbon embellishments, but in most cases, they will manipulate better if the wires are removed.

Look for the following types of woven ribbons when making ribbon embellishments.

Satin Ribbon

Satin ribbons are woven to produce a smooth, shiny finish on one side (single-faced satin) or on both sides (double-faced satin). Double-faced satin can be woven with one color on both sides or a different color on each side. Two-color double-faced ribbons can create some surprising and interesting results when the ribbon is folded and pleated. Silk satin ribbons are particularly soft and luxurious.

Feather-edge or picot satin ribbons have a fine, continuous looped thread running along each selvage, forming a decorative edge. When using them in embellishments, arrange so that the decorative loops will be seen, adding texture to the design.

Taffeta Ribbon

Taffeta ribbons have a fine, plain weave structure that is reversible. They are smooth and have a slightly lustrous surface. Taffeta ribbons can be woven plaids and checks as well as solids and variegated ombre styles that shade from dark to light or from one color to another across the width of the ribbon. Shot-effect taffetas are woven with contrasting colors in opposite directions, creating an iridescent look. Taffeta ribbons can also have a picot edge.

Grosgrain Ribbon and Petersham

In French, *gros grain* means "coarse texture." The weave structure of grosgrain ribbon creates a matte appearance and distinctive crosswise ribs. These ribbons are durable yet supple and have enough body for a crisp appearance. Today's grosgrain ribbons are usually woven from polyester.

Petersham ribbons, similar in appearance to grosgrain ribbons, are made from rayon, cotton, or a blend of fibers and can be easily pleated, folded, and gathered. Petersham ribbons, named after an eighteenth-century English lord who invented the weave, were traditionally used by milliners to decorate and finish hats. These ribbons have a slightly scalloped picot edge and are more flexible than polyester grosgrain ribbon. They can be shaped and steamed to conform to the curve of a hat band or formed in various ways to make trims and rosettes.

Jacquard Ribbon

Jacquard ribbons feature intricate, woven designs and resemble miniature tapestries. Metallic threads may be incorporated into the designs, which can include florals, geometric shapes, and other figures. Jacquards have a pronounced right and wrong side and would not be suitable for an embellishment where both sides are visible. Jacquard ribbons may also be called brocade or damask ribbons.

Sheer Ribbon

Sheer ribbons, which include organdy and georgette, are finely woven ribbons that are light and airy. They can be solid or patterned and may have satin or metallic stripes woven into the sheer. Organdy ribbons often feature a shot effect produced by weaving the ribbon from two contrasting colors so it changes appearance in reaction to the way the light falls on it. Many sheer ribbons have a monofilament woven into the selvages.

Velvet Ribbon

Like the fabric, velvet ribbons have a cut pile that is soft and luxurious to the touch and gives extra depth to their colors. Classic woven velvet ribbon has a plush pile on the front side and satin on the back. Velvet ribbons should be treated with care as the pile can be easily crushed from folding, pleating, and pressing.

Other Supplies

Needles and Pins

Use only fine, sharp pins and hand or machine needles so they do not leave holes in the ribbon. Limit your use of pins to avoid marks in the ribbon.

Thread

Good quality polyester sewing thread is available in a wide variety of colors to match any ribbon. Fine quilting thread is also a good choice.

Thread Conditioner

A light application of beeswax can make it easier to pass the thread through the ribbon and prevent it from tangling. Fabric, beading, and craft stores also carry other thread conditioners, such as Thread Heaven™,

Scissors

Use a sharp pair of scissors, dedicated to cutting fabric only, when working with ribbon. Cut wire edge and monofilament ribbons with craft scissors as they may dull your fabric shears.

Fabric Marking Pen

Pens designed for marking fabric are useful when measuring and marking ribbons. If the marked areas will show once the embellishment is made, first test the pen on the ribbon you are using to make sure that the marks can be removed. Some marking pens are "invisible" and are meant to disappear in a short period of time. Others are designed to be removed with water or heat.

Buckram

Traditionally, ribbon rosettes were constructed and sewn to buckram, a stiff, coarse material sized with glue. Buckram is traditionally used to make books and draperies and is often used to stiffen the brim of baseball caps. It is sold by the yard, and bolts can be found in the drapery section of stores that carry home decorator fabrics. Depending upon the size and type of embellishment, circles cut from buckram yardage are recommended as a base for some rosettes.

Stiff interfacing or a double layer of fused felt can be used instead of the buckram. The rosette embellishments can also be formed and sewn directly to a project.

Glue and Adhesives

Fabric glue, such as Fabri-Tac™, is made especially for fabrics and in some situations can hold ribbons together better than hand or machine stitches. Hot glue is a good choice when making ribbon sculptures as the glue sets up quickly and holds the shapes. Iron-on adhesive tape, available in various widths, fuses ribbons together with the heat of an iron.

Sealants

Fray Check™ is a liquid sealant designed to be used with fabrics to prevent raw-cut ribbon edges from fraying. Alternatively, a fine line of clear nail polish can be used. Cut ribbon ends can also be cut and sealed with a textile or wood burning heat tool. A battery operated ribbon cutter is available that uses a hot fine wire to simultaneously cut and seal ribbon ends. Synthetic ribbons work best with any type of heat tool.

Measuring Tools

Use a yardstick to measure ribbon yardage needed for an embellishment. A clear ruler is helpful when marking ribbons for pleating or folding. A small sewing gauge is also handy.

Needle-Nose Pliers or Tweezers

Small needle-nose pliers or tweezers are helpful for removing wires from wire-edge ribbon.

Sewing Machine

Most embellishments can be easily created with hand stitches. In a few cases, machine stitching can also be used.

Iron, Ironing Board, and Press Cloth

Always check the fiber content and any manufacturer care instructions on the ribbon packaging for guidance on selecting the best temperature for ironing ribbons. Placing a press cloth between the iron and the ribbon can protect the ribbon from shining or spotting.

Buttons and Beads

When making rosettes, trims, and ribbon beads, look for interesting contemporary and vintage buttons and beads to coordinate with the ribbons you select.

Pleater Board

A pleater board makes it easier to form regular narrow pleats in ribbon. First tuck the ribbon into the louvers of the board and then iron the pleats to set the folds.

Hairpin Lace Loom

A hairpin lace loom is an adjustable frame traditionally used for making crocheted hairpin lace. These looms are also very handy for making loopy ribbon fringe.

General Techniques

Ribbon Measurements

The measurements given for creating each embellishment are only a guideline. You may want to customize your embellishments and make them fuller or wider or larger, etc. For determining the exact amount of ribbon needed for any embellishment, make a small sample. Calculate the amount of ribbon needed to make that sample and use those measurements to determine the total amount of ribbon you will need for the finished embellishment. You may also want to experiment with different widths of ribbon, which will alter the final yardage needed. Different types of ribbons might be thicker or thinner and that can also change the exact yardage you will use.

Sewing with Ribbons

Most embellishments can be made with a few basic hand running stitches. To join ribbons at a seam, make the stitches small and secure both ends with a knot. When gathering ribbons, make the stitches longer so that the ribbon easily gathers up when you pull the thread. Machine stitching is an option too. When hemming the ribbon or when the stitching might show, use small slip stitches, catching just a thread or two of the ribbon with each stitch.

Whether hand or machine stitching, always use a fine, sharp needle so the holes formed will not leave marks or snag the ribbon.

Removing Wires from Wire-Edge Ribbons

Ribbons with a wire or monofilament edge can be used for making embellishments, but in many cases, the wire or filament should be removed. Test a sample piece of the ribbon to see how easily the wires can be removed and how removing the wire will change the feel of the ribbon.

With small pliers or tweezers, carefully expose the end of the wire at the cut end of the ribbon. Pull out the wire a little at a time. Slowly gather the ribbon down the wire to keep it from breaking inside the ribbon. If the wire does break, use your fingers to find the spot where the wire has broken and poke it out of the ribbon. Continue to use the pliers or tweezers to carefully remove the wire from the entire length of the ribbon. Once you've removed the wire, it may be necessary to gently iron the ribbon to smooth out any wrinkles.

Finishing Ribbon Ends

Cut ends of woven ribbons can unravel and fray. To minimize this, cut the ends at an angle or into a point or V shape.

In situations where a cut ribbon end will be exposed or the embellishment will be worn frequently or washed, it is best to seal the edges. A fine line of clear nail polish or Fray Check™ sealant can be applied along the edge. Take care to apply just a small amount and be very neat. Always test the sealant on the selected ribbon.

The cut ends of synthetic ribbon can be heat-sealed. Heat sealing will not work on natural fibers as they will not melt and they may burn. Very quickly pass the cut ribbon along the open flame of a candle or lighter. Take safety precautions when working with an open flame. It takes practice to do this so the ends do not singe and darken. The easier method for heat sealing the cut ends is to use a textile heat tool, a wood burning tool, or a battery operated ribbon cutter. All these tools will simultaneously cut and seal the ribbon. Follow the manufacturer's instructions to achieve the sealed edge.

Resources

The ribbons and supplies used to make the ribbon embellishments in this book are available through the following manufacturers.

Berwick Offray	www.BerwickOffray.com
Of The Earth	www.custompaper.com
Renaissance Ribbons	www.renaissanceribbons.com
Ribbon Connections, Inc.	www.ribbonconnections.com
Annie's Crafts	www.AnniesCatalog.com
Beacon Adhesives	www.beacon1.com
Coats & Clark	www.coatsandclark.com
Imaginisce	www.imaginisce.com
Prym Consumer USA	www.dritz.com
Simplicity Creative Group	www.Simplicity.com
therm-o-web	www.thermoweb.com

About the Author

Elaine Schmidt is a designer, consultant, educator, and spokesperson in the sewing, quilting, and craft industries. She works with leading creative industry manufacturers to develop new products, inspire consumers, and promote innovative uses for products.

Elaine has been a ribbon collector (hoarder!) since she was a child and has a few treasures in her stash that prove it. A self-described fabric, button, and bead collector; yarn and thread junkie; and sewing geek; Elaine grew up "always making something." Her mom taught her proper traditional sewing techniques, but now she enjoys bending the old-school rules a bit and "coloring outside the lines." Never happy to do one thing at a time, Elaine always has several projects in the works.

Elaine loves developing new product concepts, experimenting with traditional techniques using modern materials, and sharing ideas so others can experience the joy of working with their hands to create a project that is truly their own. She is a constant shopper and people watcher, always looking for new trends that can be translated into DIY projects.

Elaine's love of sewing led her to major in textiles and design at Carnegie Mellon University. She has worked in the education and design departments of a major sewing pattern company and is the former design director for a national chain of ribbon boutiques. Elaine is the author of *Precut Patchwork Party* and *The Complete Photo Guide to Ribbon Crafts* for Quayside Publishing. As the owner of Elaine Schmidt Designs, she has developed award-winning products for many manufacturers. Her original designs are featured in books, magazines, websites, project sheets, and TV segments, as well as on national trade and consumer sewing, quilting, and craft shows.

Elaine has three amazing daughters and lives in Long Valley, NJ with her husband, Ken, and spoiled bichon, Daisy, as well as her ever-growing stash of ribbon, fabric, thread, buttons, and all the "fun stuff."

You can catch up on her latest inspirations and projects by visiting her blog at www.elaineschmidt.com/wordpress or see the images that catch her eye on www.pinterest.com/eschmidtdesigns

Acknowledgments

Thank you to my editor Linda Neubauer and the staff at Quayside Publishing for once again giving me the opportunity to write a book about something I enjoy doing.

Thank you to all the manufacturers who so generously provided me with samples and product information to create the ribbon embellishments in this book. It is easy to make pretty things when you work with inspiring, quality products.

Thank you to my many friends who have encouraged me as I have worked my way through my list of 100 embellishments.

A big thank you to my wonderful family. You all are my very best cheerleaders and your love and laughter keep me going each day.

And a very special thank you to my husband and best friend, Kenny, who is always here to help in so many ways, whether it be IT support, photography tips, or take-out food when I just can't face the idea of cooking dinner. Your constant love and support makes everything in this crazy world make sense.

OTHER BOOKS BY ELAINE SCHMIDT

The Complete Photo Guide to Ribbon Crafts
ISBN: 978-1-58923-469-7

Precut Patchwork Party
ISBN: 978-1-58923-729-2

OTHER BOOKS IN THE SERIES

How to Make 100 Paper Flowers
Maria Noble
ISBN: 978-1-58923-751-3

How to Make 100 Crochet Appliques
Deborah Burger
ISBN: 978-1-58923-752-0

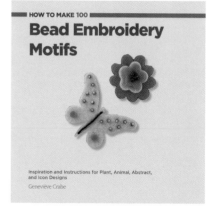

How to Make 100 Bead Embroidery Motifs
Geneviève Crabe
ISBN: 978-1-58923-779-7

OUR BOOKS ARE AVAILABLE AS E-BOOKS, TOO!

Many of our bestselling titles are now available as e-books.
Visit www.Qbookshop.com to find links to e-vendors!